Pioneer
Narratives

Cynthia Ann Parker

Cynthia Ann Parker. Tintype, ca. 1861. Courtesy Lawrence T. Jones, III.

Cynthia Ann Parker
The Life and The Legend

Margaret Schmidt Hacker

The University of Texas at El Paso

Southwestern Studies No. 92

First Edition
6 7 8 9 / 06 05 04 03

Library of Congress Catalog Card No. 89-052073
ISBN 0-87404-187-2

Cover photo: Cynthia Ann Parker. Joseph E. Taulman Collection, Barker Texas History Center, The University of Texas at Austin.

To
*Pete, Carol, Steve, Beth, Steve,
and Helen*
For Their Love and Understanding.

CONTENTS

ACKNOWLEDGMENTS

I wish to express thanks to my friends and colleagues who have made the completion of this manuscript possible. I am particularly indebted to the staff of the Fort Sill Archives, the Oklahoma Historical Society, and the Eugene C. Barker History Center. I also want to thank Dr. Light T. Cummins for the opportunity to start this project and the encouragement to continue it. Very special thanks are extended to Dr. Donald Worcester for his utmost patience and wisdom. With his guidance, this manuscript became a reality.

On a personal level, I would like to thank my friends Barbara Leahy, Bil Kerrigan, Kent Carter, Jim Kettle, Overnice Wilks, Marcia Melton, Barbara Rust, Joe Herring, Margie Jenkins, Larry Barnes, Beverly Moody, and April Coldsmith for their advice, criticism, and friendship.

Deepest thanks are extended to my family. I am forever grateful to Carol and Stephen Schmidt for their unending love. They introduced me to the world of history, spent their hard-earned money on my education, and gave me all the support a daughter could ever want. Without their support, this project would not have been possible. Very warm thanks are also due Elizabeth Dwyer and Stephen B. Schmidt for their constant encouragement and undeniable patience over the years.

Finally, I extend my appreciation to my husband, Pete, for his professional criticism and personal support. He has enabled me to enjoy and endure the pleasures and frustrations of writing this manuscript.

PREFACE

As the American frontier moved westward, many pioneer women and children were carried off by Indians. Some were later ransomed or recaptured and returned to their families. It was not unusual for boys who had been captured and raised by Indians to remain with them by choice. It was more unusual for women to prefer Indian life, but some who had been captured while young identified with a tribe so completely that they chose not to leave it. Among them was Cynthia Ann Parker. Although she never related her experiences as a Comanche captive, her story is probably the best known of all the pioneer women who were captured by Indians in the Southwest.

On the morning of 19 May 1836, during a surprise attack on Fort Parker, mounted warriors abducted nine-year-old Cynthia Ann and four other settlers. Within six years, all of the captives had been ransomed except for young Cynthia Ann. Attempts to rescue her failed because her captors were unwilling to release her. As the years passed, however, she became so thoroughly acculturated that she refused to leave the Comanches and return to white society.

In late 1860 Texas Rangers attacked a small Comanche hunting camp, killing all of its inhabitants except three, among them Cynthia Ann. She returned to the whites as unwillingly as she had left them. Having spent most of her life with Indians, Cynthia Ann found it difficult to adapt to the white society in which she had lived only nine years. Torn from her Comanche life and family, the lonely woman died only ten years after the Rangers had "rescued" her.

Since the mid-nineteenth century, many Texas folktales and legends have focused upon Cynthia Ann. Unfortunately her story has either been ignored in history books or so exaggerated and romanticized that it is difficult — if not impossible — to determine the true nature of her Comanche experiences. Problems arise when reviewing the various popular accounts of her life, for Cynthia Ann had become a legend in her own day and many whites took advantage of her name. Some of them published memoirs, letters, or articles designed to incite anti-Indian sentiment, using Cynthia Ann as a vehicle for venting their spite. Others wrote for publicity, placing themselves in the roles of various figures intersecting Cynthia Ann's life. Still others wrote historical fiction that over the years became accepted as fact. To clarify discrepancies historians must examine all accounts critically.

Cynthia Ann became a captive in two societies. Her adult life reflected Comanche culture; while whites pitied her, the Indians respected her. After the Parker raid, she had ceased to be a white girl influenced by white standards. Cynthia Ann accepted Indian tradition and custom and became thoroughly a Comanche; she even married and reared her children with her adopted people. When separated from her Indian husband, children, and friends, she thought only of returning to her Comanche family. Yet Cynthia Ann's hopes were in vain. She died in the 1870s, still isolated from the Indians.

The Capture

Many versions of Cynthia Ann Parker's life have been related in both Comanche and English. For some, the abduction of nine-year-old Cynthia Ann by "savage" Indians and her subsequent years with the Comanches were the major catastrophic events affecting her, while others viewed her forced return to white society as the real tragedy.

Because she was a captive in both the Indian and the white worlds, much of Cynthia Ann's life was truly tragic. After she was returned to white society, few pioneers understood her unhappiness over the loss of her Indian family. Most white Texans viewed her Comanche life as degrading. Almost all settlers in Texas had heard of the raid on Fort Parker in 1836 and the capture of nine-year-old Cynthia Ann and four other members of the Parker clan. After her recovery a quarter of a century later, the Texas Legislature granted her money, land, and even child support for her daughter Topsannah to compensate for her ordeal as a captive of "savage" Indians. She was offered all the comforts most white women of her time might have wanted, but without her husband and sons, her "rescue" left her more miserable than she had ever been.

Inconsistant w/ Searchers

To her adopted Indian band, Cynthia Ann was a tribal member, the respected wife of prominent chief Peta Nocona and mother of Quanah Parker, later the most sagacious Comanche chief of his day. Cynthia Ann lived with the tribe for almost twenty-five years, and their customs, habits, and ways became her own; she married, bore three children, and raised them as Comanches. In December 1860, Texas Rangers abruptly uprooted Cynthia Ann and brought her back to "civilization" where she died only ten years later. It is perhaps more ironic than symbolic that her son Quanah later helped establish peaceful relations between Comanches and whites in the Southwest.

Behind these basic facts a more complex story emerges, the significance of which has always been clouded by hearsay and exaggerated accounts of Cynthia Ann's life. By the time the Parker family reached Texas, they had followed the familiar pattern of westward migration for years. Faced with meager economic opportunities in the East, such frontier families did not hesitate to relocate in unknown regions, taking their extended families with them if there was the slightest chance for a better life.

The Parkers's background was typical of many early American families. In the late 1770s, Cynthia Ann's grandparents, John Parker and Sally White, married in Culpeper County, Virginia, near the foothills of the Blue Ridge Mountains. From this union came a line of Parkers destined to become prominent Texans. Sally and John considered themselves "two seed" Baptists, members of a branch of the Primitive Baptist Church. Firm in their religious beliefs, they led stringently pious lives and faithfully adhered to the precepts of the Bible; their children were named Daniel, Isaac, John, James, Silas, and Benjamin.

When the American Revolution ended, they found that little had changed; the large plantation owners still dominated Virginia politically, socially, and economically. Because John Parker felt that opportunities might be better in Georgia, the family moved to Elbert County in the northeastern part of that state. Thinking fortunes were to be made planting cotton, the Parkers started a farm near the Savannah River. Like most small planters, the family bought slaves to do much of the heavy work, although they did not hesitate to engage in manual labor themselves. While in Georgia, John Parker became a leader in his church, and was known as "Elder John." A restless man, he could not settle permanently anywhere. After a few years in Georgia, Elder John decided that it was time to move his family farther west — into the "wild frontier." Rumors had reached Elbert County of a new land of opportunity across the Appalachians. The Parkers packed their belongings and headed west to Tennessee some time in 1801 or 1802. They were a close family, and whenever Elder John decided to move, the whole clan went with him, including his married sons and their families. For the next twelve years, the Parkers resided in south central Tennessee near the Duck River in Bedford County.[1]

After the War of 1812, the Parkers moved again. Following the Cumberland, Ohio, and Wabash Rivers north, they settled in Clark County in east central Illinois. Elder John participated in community affairs in the area, while his oldest son Daniel became the leader of the Parkers. The family grew steadily and by the late 1820s all of John's and Sally's sons, except Benjamin, were married and had children. Elder John eventually had twenty-five grandchildren with him in Illinois, including Cynthia Ann, born to Silas and Lucy Parker in 1827.[2]

Of the many dangers settlers faced in Illinois, disease took the greatest toll. During the late 1820s, all of the Parker children contracted a fever, and three of Isaac's children died. Isaac swore that he and his family would leave Illinois as soon as possible. Soon after the death of Isaac's children, the Parkers learned of the younger John's death in a fight with the Delaware Indians near Cape Girardeau in southeast Missouri. The death of his son and Isaac's children provided an excuse to move to Texas.[3]

The area west of the Sabine River was unknown to the Parkers; they had heard of Texas only from rumors and stories about its prairies, trading posts, free frontier life, distant Mexican rule, and nomadic Indian bands.[4] They also had been informed that every married man received a grant of 4,600 acres. In the fall of 1830, James and Daniel left Illinois to take advantage of land opportunities in Texas. Daniel wanted to organize a Baptist church there, but he learned that Mexican law prohibited Protestant churches in Texas. He decided, therefore, to organize his church in Illinois and then take the forty-member congregation to the new land so that they could practice their religion as members of a single settlement rather than as an organized church. In 1832 the Parker family started their journey south.

The Parkers and the newly formed Baptist congregation traveled with twenty-five ox-drawn wagons. Travelers usually made the trip in a few months, but it took this group longer, for they refused to travel on Sundays. On those days they preached, sang, worshipped,

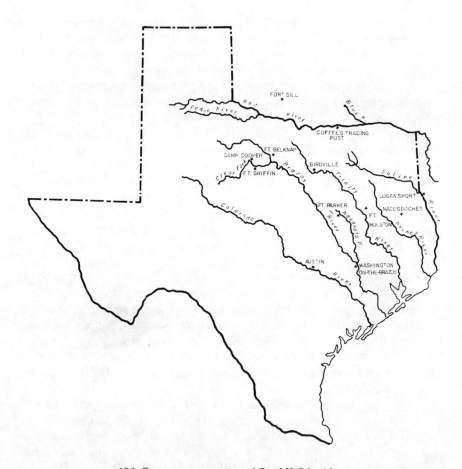

19th Century map courtesy of Carol K. Schmidt.

and celebrated in the satisfying belief that they were carrying the gospel "to the uttermost corners of the world."[5]

After passing through Missouri and Arkansas in the fall of 1832, the group mistakenly crossed the Red River east of the Texas border and passed into Louisiana. After realizing their error, they rested in Logansport before crossing the Sabine River into Texas. Local settlers told them that once across the river they should follow the trails left by Coushatta Indians. Fording the Neches, Trinity, and Navasota Rivers, they finally arrived at Stephen F. Austin's colony between the Brazos and Colorado rivers. Gathering supplies, new horses, and fresh oxen, the Parkers and the congregation stayed at Grimes Prairie, southeast of the colony, for almost a year and a half.

During the summer of 1833, Cynthia Ann's father Silas and two other members of the party traveled northwest into modern Limestone County, then part of the Robertson Colony. Each of the men staked claims to plots of land and then returned to Grimes Prairie to move their families to their new homes. They followed the Spanish trail between San Antonio and Nacogdoches to the "Old Tidwell Place." Some decided to build log cabins and establish a settlement there, while others, particularly the church members, chose to settle a few miles north in the community now known as Elkhart in present Anderson County.[6]

The remaining Parkers continued westward, reaching Fort Houston in the fall of 1833.[7] There they obtained supplies and fresh oxen before making the final part of their western trek. After crossing the Trinity River, the clan traveled forty-five miles to the headwaters of the Navasota River, where they began building Fort Parker. The winter of 1833-34 was extremely cold, but by the following spring they had finished work on their new home. Cabins were built, fields cleared, and the settlement soon appeared prosperous. By the end of 1835, thirty-four persons, including young Cynthia Ann, lived at Fort Parker. The Parker migration across the country had reached its goal.

Well planned and carefully constructed, Fort Parker included cabins, blockhouses, and a stockade. The cabins on one side of the compound were separated by divisions of wooden planks. The blockhouses were positioned at the corners of the stockade for further protection.[8] Each blockhouse had two levels; the upper rooms could be reached only by a ladder from the inside. This upper floor was larger in order to give a greater vantage point from which to defend the fort. None of the exterior walls had windows or openings lower than ten to twelve feet. These walls were specifically designed to be impossible to scale from outside the fort. The stockade itself measured ten to fifteen feet in height, with the logs sharply pointed at the top. Two observation posts were also positioned on opposite corners of the compound. The Parkers cut down all trees adjacent to the fort in order to provide greater visibility.[9]

The fort's most impressive feature was its bullet-proof gate, which the men built of thick wood slabs without using any nails or iron. They also constructed a vestibule for extra protection within the gate area. Even the overly cautious Parkers felt secure inside their impregnable compound. To maintain safety, strict rules and a rigid discipline were enforced. No one left the fort after dark and the gate remained closed and guarded at all times. If properly defended, Fort Parker could have held off a large enemy force.

During the 1830s Texas settlers were continually harassed by Comanche, Kiowa, and Caddo war parties, and hostilities were chronic in the Red River region. In 1835, the threat of Indian attacks compelled the colonists to abandon Fort Parker and seek refuge in Louisiana; but the Trinity River flooded that year, and the fleeing colonists were unable to cross. While waiting for the water to recede, they heard rumors that the Mexican dictator Antonio Lopez de Santa Anna had been defeated and Texas was free from Mexican rule. The excited colonists returned to their compound via Fort Houston, where they purchased supplies. Convinced that the threat of danger had subsided, the settlers relaxed and lessened their guard. During the summer of 1835, they often left the gate open for long periods of time, using the breeze thus created as justification for their dangerous and negligent practice.

Living inside the fort were Elder John, his wife, Sally, and their sons Benjamin, James, and Silas, together with their families. James and his wife, Martha, had six children; two of them, Rachel Plummer and Sarah Nixon, were also married and had children. Other residents included Silas's wife, Lucy, and her four children; Mrs. Nixon — mother-in-law of Sarah — and her sister, Elizabeth Kellogg; Mrs. Duty, mother of Martha and Lucy Parker; Samuel Frost and his wife and children; and G. E. Dwight and his family. Living on nearby farms were Silas Bates, David and Evan Faulkenberry, and Abram Anglin.

In October 1835, Daniel Parker proposed to create a company of Texas Rangers to protect settlers from marauding Indians. The permanent council at the "Consultation of 1835," a committee organized to direct the affairs of the Texas Revolution, accepted the proposal and named Silas Parker to command the regiment of Rangers between the Brazos and Trinity rivers. Silas wrote to the general council of Texas, "I have used my utmost exertion to raise the company and a large majority of the company is now in the woods persuent [sic] to my order."[10]

Silas and his Rangers attacked any Indian they met, so it is likely they provoked hostility among peaceful bands in the area. Near Grimes Prairie many whites noticed that the Indians were friendly until a small number of unknown settlers tried to steal their horses. According to Daniel Parker, some whites had killed several Caddos during the spring of 1835 and a number of their tribesmen were now on the "war path." In the following year, an Indian neighbor, Jinee Jim, had told Daniel that there were five hundred Indians gathering near "Grofs' Timbers" on the Trinity River. Among them were reportedly two captive white women and some children, but the Parkers made no attempt to determine the truth of this rumor.[11]

On the morning of 19 May 1836, James W. Parker, L. D. Nixon, and Luther Plummer left Fort Parker for their fields a mile away. At approximately nine o'clock, someone within the fortress cried, "Indians! Indians!" and everyone within the fort came out and saw several hundred Indians entering the clearing.[12] Sarah Nixon ran to the fields to warn the men; at the same time, Elder John, his wife, and Elizabeth Kellogg tried to escape through an adjacent farm. Everyone anticipated great trouble. As G. E. Dwight started to leave with his family, Silas reportedly exclaimed, "Good Lord, Dwight, you are not a going to run! Stand and fight like a man, and if we have to die we will sell our lives as dear as we can!"[13] Dwight tried to explain that he was going to hide his family in the woods and would certainly return to help. Amidst all of the commotion and chaos, Benjamin left the compound to speak to the Indians assembled outside the fort.

The Indians, mostly Caddos, Comanches, and Kiowas, met Benjamin with a white flag and signs of friendship. They told him that they needed beef and directions to a waterhole; they also explained that they wanted to make peace with the new colonists. Benjamin returned to the fort and repeated the conversation, but he also expressed his fear that the Indians intended to attack. He remarked that the requests did not make any sense. Why would they be looking for a waterhole when they had just come from the direction of the Navasota River and their horses appeared wet?

Benjamin did not take time to contemplate the Indians' requests further; instead, he gathered meat and other staples in the vain hope of pacifying them with food.[14] Silas tried to stop his brother from leaving the fort, but Benjamin was determined to negotiate. Watching his brother leave, Silas reportedly told his niece Rachel, "I know that they will kill Benjamin." The Indians gathered around Benjamin, and in front of the shocked observers in the fort, they clubbed, speared, and scalped him. Then they charged upon the fort which was defenseless because the gate had been left open. The five men, ten women, and fifteen children, powerless against the Indians, attempted to leave the fort to secure protection for their families. Within half an hour the assault was over.

At the start of the onslaught, Rachel Plummer — approximately three months pregnant — and her two-year-old son James tried to escape through the rear exit of the fort. Rachel later described her capture in her autobiography: "As I passed the corner of the Fort I was in sight of the Indians, and I saw them stabbing their spears into Uncle Benjamin, and shooting him with their arrows." As Rachel attempted to leave the compound, several Indians intercepted her. "One large sulky looking Indian picked up a hoe and knocked me down. I well recollect their tearing my little James Pratt out of my arms, but whether they hit me anymore I know not." The next thing Rachel remembered was her captors dragging her by her hair. "I heard a desperate screaming near the place where they had first taken me, I heard one or two shots, and am confident that I heard uncle Silas shout a most triumphant huzza, as tho' he had thousands to back him."[15]

She was taken to the main body of Indians, her face and clothes covered with blood from the wounds made by the hoe. "I looked round for my little James Pratt, but could not see him — I expected they had killed him. . .I now looked at the place where uncle Benjamin was, and found him fully dead." Because of Rachel's persistent crying, two Comanche women tried to make her stop, and one struck her several times with a leather whip.[16]

After the Indians seized Rachel, they launched their assault on the fort, killing Silas, Samuel Frost, and his son Robert, who were the only men left in the compound to defend the women and children. Meanwhile, Elder John, his wife Sally, and Elizabeth Kellogg were overtaken three-quarters of a mile away and stripped of their clothing. William Jackson of Groesbeck recalled the story Abram Anglin told him about the death of Elder John and the subsequent events. The Indians killed him with a tomahawk, then tried to force his wife to watch them scalp him. Sally Parker would look for a while, then when the Indians started, she would turn her head. They slapped her and made her observe them. Finally after the bloody act was completed, the Indians placed both Sally Parker and Elizabeth Kellogg on horses with warriors. After about a mile, Sally purposely fell off the horse. As she lay on the ground, a warrior lanced her until he thought she was dead. The Indians kept Elizabeth Kellogg captive and rode on.[17]

By this time, Sarah Nixon had reached the fields and alerted James Parker and Luther Plummer of the attack. Her father immediately hurried for the fort, while Plummer ran to another field to warn L. D. Nixon and their neighbors, including Abram Anglin and Evan and David Faulkenberry. James found his family before reaching the compound and concealed them in the brush. While on his way to the fort, Nixon found Lucy Parker. Her husband Silas had just been killed, and she was trying to escape with her four children. Within a few minutes, several Indians surrounded them and forced them to surrender two of the children. Threatened with a tomahawk, Lucy was compelled to place her two oldest children, Cynthia Ann and John, behind mounted warriors. One group of Indians then took Nixon, Lucy, and her two children, Silas, Jr., and Orlena, back to the fort, while the others rode off with the captives.

At the fort, the Indians were about to kill Nixon when David Faulkenberry opened fire on them. The warriors immediately threw up their shields and left for a safer place. One Indian, however, charged at Lucy and came so close that her dog bit his horse's nose, causing the animal to throw its rider.

The other men from the fields arrived at the compound and immediately started searching for family members. Plummer, unable to locate Rachel and their child, took Abram's butcher knife and left the fort to search for his family. Nixon tried to locate James Parker, hoping to find his wife with him. Meanwhile, Parker, with his family and Sarah Nixon, encountered the Dwight family hiding in the thicket along the river and joined them.

David Faulkenberry and Lucy Parker also left the fort, she with one infant in her arms and holding the other by the hand. While they searched for other refugees, the Indians continued to harass them, but whenever Faulkenberry leveled his rifle, they withdrew.

Silas Bates, Abram Anglin, and Evan Faulkenberry stayed at the fort. Faced with the armed trio, the remaining Indians retreated. Planning to go for aid, the three men loaded horses with meal, bacon, and honey. They soon caught up with David Faulkenberry and Lucy. None of them knew of the whereabouts of James Parker and his party or knew that the Dwight family was with them.

That evening, several hours after the attack, Anglin and Evan Faulkenberry returned to the fort in search of survivors. As they passed Faulkenberry's cabin, they thought they saw an apparition inside. Anglin described it as a white figure with long stringy hair motioning for the two men to come closer. It turned out to be the severely wounded Sally Parker, who had crawled from the fields all the way to the Faulkenberry cabin. Anglin set up a bed for her before the two men continued their search. At the compound they discovered no sign of life other than the dogs, cattle, horses, and pigs. Sally had told them where she had hidden $106.50 in silver, which they recovered near a hickory tree. The trauma of the day gripped them with fear and they did not stay long. Finding no survivors, they returned to Sally Parker and rejoined the rest of their party. The next morning, Faulkenberry's party, including Sally Parker, departed for Fort Houston on horseback.

James Parker was unaware of the existence of any survivors other than those in his own party. This group consisted of himself, his wife, and their children; Mrs. Frost and her children; and G. E. Dwight, his wife, mother-in-law, and children — making a total of eighteen people. Twelve of them were children ranging from infancy to twelve years. Panic stricken, they decided to walk to Fort Houston, almost 150 miles from their abandoned settlement. Barefooted, bareheaded, and dressed in rags, they plodded slowly along the river bank, under continual observation by the Indians on the high cliffs lining the river.

Frightened and grief-stricken, the party traveled cautiously at night and hid in thickets during the day. James Parker wrote in his narrative of the journey that "every few steps, did I see the briars tear the legs of the little children until the blood trickled down so that they could have been tracked by it."[18] Suffering from hunger and fatigue, they stopped frequently, which delayed their progress. The only food they had for the first two days, was one skunk. Four days later they killed another skunk and two small terrapins. By the next day the women and children could not travel any farther. At this point, James left the group and walked the rest of the way alone. He was amazed that he covered the thirty-mile journey in only eight hours. He had not eaten in six days, for he had given his small share of the food to his children.

Exhausted, James arrived at Fort Houston on 24 May. A Captain Carter welcomed him and offered assistance. The next day, Carter and two officers returned for the fugitives and brought them to Fort Houston where they received medical attention and contacted other family members who had settled in the area. On the following day, Plummer arrived at the same settlement, assuming that his wife, child, and all others from Fort Parker were dead.

On 28 May Nixon's group arrived at Fort Houston. Learning that James Parker and his party were at the settlement, Nixon joined them and informed authorities that at least five persons had been killed and five captured during the raid. On 19 June James and a few others returned to Fort Parker to bury the dead. Sally Parker had died shortly after reaching Fort Houston and was taken back to Fort Parker for burial. James recalled that "We made a rough box, into which we deposited their remains, (except those of my youngest brother, which I preserved, as he and I had entered into an agreement, that whichever survived, should see that his brother's body was not buried), and having dug a grave, they were buried."

There was not much for the group to recover, for "the crops were entirely destroyed, the horses stolen, nearly all the cattle killed, and not a single article of household furniture left." The burial party also tried to determine the route the Indians had taken with the captives, but found few traces. Having searched in vain, they returned to Fort Houston.[19]

It is not clear as to who provoked the attack on Fort Parker. Silas and his Texas Rangers may have incited various tribes to retaliate against the fort, or perhaps the Indians launched the assault to hinder white settlers from advancing further into their territory. The attack, nevertheless, ended the westward migration of the Parker clan and their hopes for a prosperous farming community. The survivors started life anew; some moved away from the Fort Parker area, while others cultivated new farms in the vicinity. James Parker immediately began a search for his daughter and the other captives. For one member of the family a totally different way of life began; young Cynthia Ann had virtually entered another world. By the time members of her family saw her again they would barely recognize her for she was no longer a nine-year-old white girl but an adult Comanche woman.

what about uncle Ethan

The Captivity

After setting fire to the Parkers' fields and outbuildings and killing many of their cattle, the Caddos, Comanches, and Kiowas took their five new captives away from Fort Parker. As one of the prisoners later recalled, the war party split up into small groups soon after the raid to make any pursuit difficult. They rode until midnight, when the Indians made camp on the open prairie. Then for the first time, the Indians brought the captives together. With their hands and feet tied behind them, the prisoners were thrown on the ground, kicked, and beaten. The Indians reenacted the raid in dance form, shouting, flourishing the fresh scalps, and striking the captives with their bows. They were all abused, even eighteen-month-old James Pratt Plummer, whose cries for his mother diminished as the child began to weaken from the beatings he received. Elizabeth Kellogg, Rachel Plummer, and John and Cynthia Ann Parker were all helpless against the harsh and painful punishments inflicted upon them.[1]

In the days which followed, the group traveled north through prairies interspersed with woods, crossing many rivers that were unfamiliar to the captives. The Indians refused to tell them where they were going or what would be their eventual fate. For several nights the Indians continued dancing, singing, and abusing their prisoners. They gave their captives no food for five days and only small amounts of water. On the sixth day they reached the Grand Prairie and divided the captives. The Kichais received Elizabeth Kellogg, while different Comanche bands took the others.

The treatment of the captives taken at Fort Parker was typical of the fate of many Indian prisoners. Some were mistreated or killed; others were adopted into the tribe. It was not unusual for white captives to adapt completely to tribal ways, but the degree of assimilation depended upon the captive's age, personality, and the duration of captivity. Because men proved less submissive and required more supervision, Indians rarely took them prisoners. Captives were considered public property when their masters were away; at such times they were occasionally abused. Owners of captives exercised complete control over them. The captives could be sold, given to other Indians, enslaved, or even married to a tribe member.[2]

Only Cynthia Ann, of all the Fort Parker captives, assimilated completely to Comanche life. Except for the first week, her experiences from the time of her captivity to her return to white society are not completely known, but her early treatment was probably similar to that of other captives. Elizabeth Kellogg told James Parker little about her own captivity, and related only sketchy information about the Indians who raided Fort Parker. Rachel Parker Plummer wrote a short but detailed account of her year with the Indians, but her experiences were probably different from Cynthia Ann's because of her maturity. John Parker and James Pratt Plummer were small children at the time of their capture; they were ransomed in 1842 after six years among the Indians and little is known of their treatment or degree of assimilation to Comanche life. Because Cynthia Ann seldom spoke of her twenty-five years with the Indians, the accounts of the other four captives must be considered to draw conclusions about her life among the Comanches.

The Kichais ransomed Elizabeth Kellogg to some Delawares for $150, who after a few months delivered her to General Sam Houston in Nacogdoches and were reimbursed. On 20 August 1836 James W. Parker met her there and they departed for his new home about fifty miles from Fort Houston. On the way, they met a traveler named Smith who had just seen two Indians trying to steal his horses and had shot one of them. Parker recalled that "we found that Mr. Smith had partially missed his aim, for the ball had merely grazed his [the Indian's] forehead." Elizabeth believed the wounded man was the one who had scalped Elder John, adding that he would have scars on both arms if he were the same person. Parker examined the Indian "with mingled feelings of joy, sorrow, and revenge, [finding] the scars as described: — joy at the opportunity of avenging the butchery of my father, and sorrow at the recollection of it." Elizabeth explained that this man had taken her from the fort and had left her with his tribe while he went on another war party. The Indian was apparently surprised to see Elizabeth "at liberty and with her friends." After killing the Indian, Parker and Smith declared with satisfaction that this murderer "would never kill and scalp another white man."[3]

Elizabeth was unable to give Parker any information regarding the other captives. Still hoping to locate and ransom them, he left in late September for Coffee's trading post several hundred miles away on the Red River. There on 2 October, Parker learned that a white woman fitting Rachel Plummer's description had been brought to a Captain Pace's post on the Blue River, a tributary of the Red River. When Parker arrived at Pace's, some of Coffee's traders were there who informed him that his daughter Rachel was "in [the] charge of a band of Indians," who were camped near the trading post. They also told him that the Indians had killed her son James Pratt. Parker immediately departed for the camp, but by the time he arrived the Indians had already left. He was unable to track them, and returned home in mid-November with no further information about his daughter or the other captives.[4]

Rachel Plummer stayed with the Indians a year before traders ransomed her. In her account of her capture, *Narrative of 21 Months Servitude As a Prisoner Among the Comanche Indians*, she gave a vivid description of her feelings, surroundings, and everyday life from the attack on Fort Parker until she was reunited with her family in 1838. Her experiences of enslavement echoed those of other white captives. The pattern of their day to day existence varied in specifics more than essentials.

According to Rachel's story, the Comanches brought her son to her on the fourth day of captivity because they did not know if he was still being breast-fed. Covered with bruises and bleeding wounds, the baby was in poor condition. Rachel embraced her son, but the Indians tore him away from his mother's arms when they realized that James had been weaned. Her last memory of the child was as he stretched "forth his little bloody hands towards me."[5] During July and August 1836, the Indians moved their camp into some snow-covered mountains. Rachel had no shoes or covering for her feet and little clothing. At night the Indians burned buffalo chips to keep the fires going. Rachel's duties included dressing buffalo hides and tending the horses during the cold nights, but she rarely complained for fear of being beaten, a punishment often inflicted upon her.

Rachel recalled that the Indians moved their camp to an area near a lake which produced many pounds of salt. There she was given to an old woman who constantly beat her. She finally grabbed the woman's club, knocked her down, and continued beating her until others noticed the fighting and ran toward them. Rachel felt certain they would kill her; instead, the Indians patted her on the shoulder and praised her. From then on, the Comanches treated her with more respect.[6]

According to Rachel, various bands gathered in 1837 at the head of the Arkansas River. After three days, a council agreed to attack Texas and drive the settlers from the region. If they were successful, they planned to give captured farmlands to tribes who raised corn and the prairies to the hunting bands. Each group would defend the other against whites.[7] The Indians felt that with Texas in their possession they would gain many adherents in Mexico and eventually conquer that nation. The tentative date for the plan's execution was the spring of 1838 or 1839. At the council, one Indian told her that all whites would soon become servants of the Indians; he then cursed her in English — the only English words she had heard since Fort Parker.

Rachel described other Comanche traditions as well as the tribe's medical practices. They attributed death to the mismanagement of the healing rituals and life to their successful completion. They also regarded whites as their natural enemies and claimed that they had a right to enslave and torture their captives. Comanche men considered women as servants; they hunted the game, but the women had to cut and dry the meat, dress the skins, and make moccasins and clothing. Women also herded, saddled, packed, unpacked, and unsaddled the horses, and erected and dismantled tipis, along with many other tasks. Comanche women sometimes took part in tribal ceremonies and dances, but only on rare occasions.

In the early spring of 1838, the Indians ransomed Rachel to Santa Fe traders.[8] William Donoho financed her purchase and took Rachel to Santa Fe, a seventeen-day ride from the Indians' camp in the Rocky Mountains. She stayed with Donoho until her health improved, then accompanied the Donoho family to Independence, Missouri. There she met her brother-in-law, L. D. Nixon, who took her to Texas. On 19 February 1838 she reached her father's house in Montgomery County, and was reunited with her husband. Tragically, Rachel Plummer died exactly one year later, never learning the fate of her son James Pratt or the other captives.

In the summer of 1842, James Parker journeyed to a trading post on the Red River seeking the remaining captives. He had been informed by "respectable persons" that during the previous spring several Comanches and members of other tribes had asked traders to inform the Texas government that they wanted to negotiate peace and deliver their white captives. "Believing that if peace [was] established between these tribes and the Texians . . . their trade would be broken up," the traders told the Indians that the Texans did not want peace "but were determined to wage a war of extermination against them." Many settlers believed that the Indians were so exasperated by this response that they were preparing to renew hostilities. According to the *Houston Telegraph and Texas Register*, these traders "are carrying on a very lucrative traffic with the Indians who are hostile to Texas, and it is possible that the desire for pelf may have induced them even to barter away the lives of our frontier citizens."[9] In this atmosphere of increased distrust, Parker was unable to obtain any information from the Indians about the captives.

After six years of captivity among different tribes, James Pratt Plummer was ransomed by the army and taken to Fort Gibson in 1842. With the help of U. S. Indian agents and the Republic of Texas, in 1843 he reached his grandfather's house in Anderson County. He lived in Anderson and Houston counties until his death late in the nineteenth century.[10]

When Parker met his grandson at Fort Gibson, he also found his nephew John Parker, who supposedly was ransomed by the same agents. In a letter to Secretary of the Treasury William Henry Daingerfield, dated 10 December 1842, Sam Houston stated that he had authorized seventy-five dollars to James Parker for "the redemption of Captives from the Indians" and the release of his nephew "now in possession of the command of Genl. Taylor, in command of the U.S. Troops on our frontier."[11] This advance was in addition to an earlier appropriation of $200 for John's ransom, or for the person who ransomed him. No one raised any money on Cynthia Ann's behalf; but Parker claimed to have made three earlier trips — all fruitless — into Indian territory searching for her as well as the other captives.

The most popular story of John and the Comanches is that John was raised with Indian boys and eventually became a hunter and warrior. According to this myth, he raided mainly in Mexico and southern Texas, and achieved distinction in the tribe. On one long raid he caught smallpox, and because of a plague which had earlier swept the plains area, the Indians immediately abandoned him with a newly-captured young Mexican woman named Juanita whom he later married. The two returned to Mexico, where they remained until the Civil War. John enlisted in the Confederate Army, but refused to cross into Louisiana and returned to Mexico.[12] This romantic account was widely accepted even though Houston's letter indicates that he had, in fact, been ransomed. In 1844, James Parker wrote Mirabeau B. Lamar that of the five Fort Parker captives, "only Sinthy ann [sic] remains in captivity."[13]

Assuming that Cynthia Ann's treatment was similar to that of the others, one may conjecture about her life among the Comanches. No appropriations had been made for Cynthia Ann's ransom and only through the legends of the attack on Fort Parker did anyone know of the young captive. White Texans heard nothing of Cynthia Ann until the spring of 1840, when Col. Leonard Williams, another trader, and an Indian guide named Jack Henry, met with Comanches camped on the Canadian River. As Williams talked with Chief Pahauka, he saw a white girl and learned that she was Cynthia Ann. He tried to purchase her release, but despite the chief's willingness, the band's council refused to accept the ransom. Williams raised his offer to twelve mules and several hundred dollars' worth of merchandise, but the Comanches declared that they would rather fight than part with her. As tempers flared, the chief intervened to prevent violence. Although the Comanches demanded that Williams leave their camp, Pahauka allowed him to speak with Cynthia Ann.[14]

While Cynthia Ann sat under a tree, staring at the ground, Williams attempted to ask her several questions, but the young woman refused to answer. He continued to talk, explaining that her mother thought she was dead, but Cynthia Ann still did not reply. Williams noticed that her lips quivered as she fought to control her emotions, and he conjectured that she had either forgotten English or the Comanches had warned her not to speak to him. Williams did not consider that she might have acculturated so rapidly to Comanche ways that she did not wish to leave. If she had received treatment similar to that of Rachel Plummer, Cynthia Ann may have been afraid to speak with Williams, but it is more likely that she had been well treated and had acculturated. Frustrated, Williams returned to the settlements where he relayed information of the captive to the Parker family.[15]

Five years after Williams' encounter with Cynthia Ann, federal agents spotted her among Comanches on the Washita River in Oklahoma. In September 1845, Commissioner of Indian Affairs William Medill instructed P. M. Butler and M. G. Lewis to gather information on the Indians of Texas and the Southwest. On their expedition, they found three captive white children, including a young man named Lyons who refused to leave the Comanches. Other captives included a seventeen-year-old girl and her ten-year-old brother who were living among the Yamparika Band on the Washita. The Yamparikas referred to them as the Parker children. Butler and Lewis reported that a warrior had claimed the young woman as his wife and "from the influence of her alleged husband, or from her own inclination, she is unwilling to leave the people with whom she associates."[16] The band seemed willing to surrender her and Butler and Lewis offered a large quantity of goods and four or five hundred dollars, "but the offer was unavailing, as she would run off and hide herself to avoid those who went to ransom her."[17] Unable to secure her release, Butler and Lewis returned to the settlements. It is impossible to determine whether the children they met were indeed the Parkers. The timing of the expedition also does not correspond with the date of Parker's letter to Lamar in 1844 after John had been ransomed. The young woman's age and reaction to Butler and Lewis's offer, however, are similar to Cynthia Ann's and her acculturated state.

Following Butler and Lewis's visit, Indian agents heard rumors of Cynthia Ann's whereabouts, but all attempts to ransom her failed. The Comanches claimed she stayed with them by her own choice, and according to the Indians, after a few years of captivity, Cynthia Ann had entered fully into tribal life and was treated like any other Comanche woman. She helped to erect tipis, dried and stored meat, prepared skins, and decorated clothing.[18]

During the 1840s Cynthia Ann had married Peta Nocona, a young warrior famous for leading the Fort Parker attack and many other victorious raids. Their marriage was apparently successful, for Nocona treated his wife considerately and she returned his affection. She was his only wife, although prominent warriors sometimes married two or three women. Nocona may have remained monogamous because of his affection for Cynthia Ann, although she might have appreciated a second wife to help her with the work. The marriage eventually produced two sons, Quanah and Pecos, and a daughter, Topsannah.

In another speculative story, Cynthia Ann's brother John reportedly visited her several years after she married. At his mother's request, he returned to Comanche country to "rescue" his sister. According to some accounts, Parker found the camp and implored Cynthia Ann to return home, but she explained that she knew no family except her adopted Indian parents, that she loved her husband, children, and friends, and could not leave them.[19]

James Parker's search for Cynthia Ann continued. Early in the spring of 1844, he heard of a young white woman who had been released from Indian captivity in Jasper County, Missouri. Hoping that she was his niece, Parker immediately departed for the area. A year later, in a letter to the editor of the *Washington-on-the-Brazos Texas National Register*, he stated that the young woman was not Cynthia Ann. The girl was about eleven or twelve years old with dark hair, brown eyes, and dark complexion, but she could not identify herself or speak any English. "I wish to make this public, because I know from experience the anxiety of the bereaved, and wish as far as lies in my power, to alleviate distress," Parker wrote.[20] He appealed to Indian agents and traders to help settlers find family members among various tribes, "I have spared neither my purse nor my person . . . and so long as I have one acre of land, or one cow, and health and strength, I shall not give it [the search] up."[21]

After Parker's fruitless venture to Missouri, an article appeared in the *Houston Telegraph and Texas Register* in 1847 stating that "Miss Parker . . . has married an Indian Chief and is so wedded to the Indian mode of life, that she is unwilling to return to her white kindred." This account added that family, traders, and federal agents had made every possible effort to reclaim her, but they had all been unsuccessful since she refused to listen to any of their "generous offers" and fled with her husband to the prairies. "Even if she should be restored to her kindred here," the article concluded, "she would probably take advantage of the first opportunity, and flee away to the wilds of northern Texas."[22]

One year after the publication of the newspaper article, another attempt to rescue Cynthia Ann was made. In 1847 Special Indian

Agent Robert S. Neighbors learned that she was with the Tenawish
Comanches. He wrote Commissioner Medill that he had used all the
means in his power during the past summer to induce those Indians
to bring her in, including large rewards, and that "it would be an act
of humanity, if the Department could restore her to her friends." He
described Cynthia Ann as being about eighteen years of age and was
assured by the "friendly Comanche Chiefs" that he would have "to
use force to induce the party that has her to give her up." The Tenawish
band lived along the Red River and had little contact with Texas
agents. Apparently Indian agents made no further attempts to ransom
her from this tribe.[23]

In 1851 a group of traders led by Victor Rose allegedly saw Cynthia
Ann while visiting a Comanche village. When they asked her to leave
with them, "she shook her head in a sorrowful negative," and pointed
to her children saying, "I am happily married; I love my husband,
who is good and kind, and my little ones, who, too, are his, and I
cannot forsake them." Rose uncharitably described Peta Nocona as a
"great, greasy, lazy buck."[24]

Many have disputed Rose's account, especially Laura Neda
Birdsong, Cynthia Ann's granddaughter. If he had indeed talked to
Cynthia Ann, they would certainly have spoken in Comanche, which
he as a trader probably understood. Her expressions of devotion to
her Indian family, if she made them, were undoubtedly sincere.[25]

The Cynthia Ann whom Rose may have met was a different person
from the little girl captured at Fort Parker fifteen years earlier. Unlike
Rachel Plummer and Elizabeth Kellogg, the nine-year-old captive had
been young enough to assimilate completely into Comanche society.
The transition between the two cultures must have been difficult at
first, especially knowing that the Comanches had killed her father,
but the Indian captors accepted Cynthia Ann as an integral part of
the band. Despite offers of large sums of money, they refused to
release her into white society.

The
Pease River Massacre

The efforts of Williams, Lewis, Butler, Parker, Neighbors, and Rose to "rescue" or ransom Cynthia Ann failed, and as the years passed, she seemed destined to fade into the mists of history alongside such figures as Virgina Dare. As Indian relations with Texans grew worse, attempts to locate Cynthia Ann ceased. The Pease River campaign of 1860 was one of many incidents during the Comanche warfare in Texas which did not reflect well upon its participants. Had Cynthia Ann not been involved, it would probably have been quickly forgotten.

During the middle decades of the nineteenth century, Indian-white warfare flared along the Texas frontier. In response, during 1838 and 1839 the Texas Legislature formulated plans for a system of frontier forts in the Southwest to be garrisoned by over a thousand soldiers. Settlers welcomed the plan and many volunteered to assist in organizing these forces. The Comanches, meanwhile, resented the gradual encroachment of whites on their hunting grounds and continued their raids. In 1840 Texas President Mirabeau B. Lamar announced his determination to drive all Indians out of Texas.[1] Reflecting Lamar's attitude, the Texans launched punitive expeditions, attacking any Indians they found, even peaceful tribes.

Ironically relations between the Comanches and whites seemed to improve in early 1840 when a band of southern Comanches made peaceful overtures to the Texans. On 9 January three Comanche chiefs met with Texas Ranger Col. Henry Wax Karnes in San Antonio to discuss a peace treaty between the two sides. Karnes declared that no peace would be possible until the Indians returned all of their white captives. Two months later, sixty-five Comanches gathered in a San Antonio council house to sign the treaty. After they delivered a young white girl named Matilda Lockhart and a few Mexican captives, Lt. Col. William S. Fisher ordered a company of soldiers to seize the Indians as hostages until other white captives were surrendered. When one Comanche tried to escape, a trooper killed him and a one-sided battle ensued. When the fighting ended, thirty-five Indians, including three women and two children, were dead and twenty-seven captured. In response to the "Council House Massacre," other southern Comanche bands increased their raiding along the frontier, and killed thirteen white prisoners held by the tribe. Throughout the 1840s, Comanches remained wary of the federal government's overtures and parleys.[2]

Although Sam Houston returned to the presidency of the Republic of Texas in 1841, the Comanches continued to view Texans as enemies, and communication between the two groups remained rare. Houston tried to win the Indians' confidence, and after several meetings a tenuous peace was secured. He authorized the establishment of trading posts on the frontier to provide goods for tribal needs. Although Houston's peace policy opened communication with some Indians, it did not win their confidence. Meanwhile, most Texans continued to favor Lamar's aggressive policy more than they approved of Houston's attempts at pacification.

During the late 1840s, the southern Comanches faced other problems. Smallpox swept through various bands in 1848 and cholera struck the tribe during the following year. Several hundred warriors died and the loss threatened the Comanches' traditional political system. Since their defensive ability also had been severely weakened, the tribe held a general council to discuss their relations with the Americans. The majority decided to negotiate for peace with both the United States and Texas, but a militant minority opposed the peace and Comanche leaders were unable to prevent these young men from continuing their raids against Texas. The federal government, therefore, refused to make peace treaties granting them permanent rights to their lands.

In the late 1840s and 1850s, the United States government established many forts throughout the Southwest to protect settlers from Indian raids and to serve as base camps for military expeditions against hostile tribes. One of the posts was Fort Belknap, built in 1852 but abandoned during the spring of 1859. In 1854 the U. S. government selected twelve leagues of land on the upper Big Wichita and Brazos rivers to create two reservations for some Comanches and various remnant tribes who were "suffering with extreme hunger bordering on starvation."[3] The Comanche reserve was located on the Clear Fork of the Brazos, approximately forty miles west of Fort Belknap. In 1855 troops also were stationed at Camp Cooper on the new Comanche reserve.[4]

Vigorous efforts by ex-Indian agent John R. Baylor to eliminate the reservations were a major factor in the deterioration of Indian-white relations in the latter 1850s. The commissioner of Indian Affairs had dismissed Baylor for unsatisfactory performance of duty. Infuriated, Baylor sought revenge, rarely missing an opportunity to discredit either Supervising Agent Robert S. Neighbors or the Indians under Neighbors's charge. He claimed that the Comanches on the Clear Fork and the remnant tribes of the Brazos Rivers reservation were committing depredations in north-central Texas and that Neighbors was protecting them. Baylor played on the emotions of whites who had lost relatives or had property destroyed in Indian raids, and he appealed to frontier riffraff who were eager to kill Indians. His purpose was to arouse settlers to the point that they would attack the reservations and kill or drive away all the Indians and agents.[5]

The inaccuracy of Baylor's accusations mattered little to aroused settlers eager to resort to violence. Neighbors feared for the safety of the Indians, especially when twenty-one men from Erath County attacked Choctaw Tom's peaceful hunting party camped near Keechi Creek on the Brazos in December 1858. They killed three women and four men and severely wounded five others. Although Neighbors knew the identity of most of the attackers, no one, not even veteran ranger Capt. John Salmon "Rip" Ford, dared to arrest them. Peter Farland, leader of the group, declared that they had the total support of local settlers and had "no apology to offer for what we have done."[6] Because other whites continued to threaten the Indians, Neighbors desperately sought assistance from the federal government.

In June 1859, after repeated requests by Neighbors, the Commissioner of Indian Affairs finally agreed that the best solution was to move the reservation Indians to Indian Territory away from irate whites. On 26 June Neighbors and agent Shapley Ross, with a military force under Major George Thomas, escorted the Wacos, Tonkawas, Tawakonis, Caddos, Anadarkos, and other remnant tribes to Fort Arbuckle in Indian Territory. Comanche Agent Mathew Leeper and other troops escorted the Clear Fork reserve Comanches to the same destination. Removing the reservation Indians, however, brought no peace to the frontier. Nonreservation Comanches in West Texas, especially Peta Nocona's band, continued their devastating raids in the region.

In the fall, Peta Nocona led several raids into Young, Jack, and Parker counties, looting farms and ranches and killing settlers.[7] Nocona and his warriors knew the area well enough to conduct their attacks at night. Whites in the region panicked and appealed to Gov. Sam Houston for aid and protection. As the raids continued, Houston authorized Col. Middleton T. Johnson to raise a ranger regiment to protect frontier settlers. Johnson failed, however, to thwart Peta Nocona's warriors.[8] His failure induced many other Texans to volunteer their services as rangers. On Houston's orders, Capt. Lawrence Sullivan Ross raised an additional forty volunteers and Capt. Nathan G. Evans, commander at Camp Cooper, "loaned" him twenty regular troops of the 2nd Cavalry, giving Ross a total of sixty men.[9]

Despite Ross's troops, Peta Nocona and his followers continued their raids in Jack and Palo Pinto counties during the fall of 1860. Women occasionally accompanied the warriors, and Cynthia Ann may have been present on some of these raids. The Comanches attacked the Rilly and Sherman homes in Parker County, killing and scalping the occupants and stealing their possessions.

Ross, his rangers, and twenty cavalrymen pursued the Comanches toward the Pease River. In early December, Captain Jack Cureton and over ninety volunteers from Bosque County also joined the expedition. The troops and volunteers reached the west bank of the river in six days. Early on the morning of 18 December 1860, Ross and twenty-five men left their camp to scout the immediate vicinity. When they found a trail that led to a prominent position overlooking the surrounding area, Ross sent word to Cureton to bring up his men.

Meanwhile Ross and his party sighted a small Comanche camp and Ross ordered his men to prepare for a fight. Shortly before the attack, Ross promised that he would present a Colt revolver to the first man who killed and scalped an Indian. He later took "great pleasure" in communicating to General Houston his report of the onslaught near the Pease River. "The Indians, unconscious of our presence, had gotten out on a level plane [*sic*]," wrote Ross, "and were never apprised of our approach until we were within 200 yards of them, in full charge, consequently many of them were killed before they could make any preparation for defense."[10]

The traditional account of the ensuing fight provided by Ross and a few others, has been contradicted by many sources.[11] According to that tradition, there were the "usual killings" as the rangers and regulars attacked the Comanches, shooting at every Indian they encountered. Ross ordered twelve rangers to intercept any fleeing Indians, and within minutes they had surrounded the area. A few of the remaining Comanches made a circle in front of Ross's men, then they dismounted, and using their horses as shields, covered those trying to escape.

Ranger Benjamin Franklin Gholson recalled that one Comanche called out for each warrior to save himself. A few Indians mounted their horses and rode two miles before the rangers caught and killed them. Ross and Lt. Tom Kelliher chased two mounted figures, one with another rider behind him. Ross reported that Kelliher, desiring a single-handed fight, pursued the lone rider for a few miles. But as he raised his gun to fire, the rider, a female, held up a baby and reportedly cried, "Americano!"[12]

Ross followed the Comanches who were riding double and fired at them, killing one. As the slain Comanche fell off the horse, he pulled the other rider down. As Ross approached he discovered that the dead "warrior" was really a young girl, but that the other Comanche was an adult male, whom Ross then shot in the arm.

Meanwhile, Antonio Martinez, Ross's servant, also approached on horseback, and since the Mexican understood the Comanche language, he translated for the captain. The wounded warrior, Martinez claimed, was Peta Nocona, who wanted his "gekovak" (god) to "give his token if he has done his duty as a chieftain."[13] Through his translator, Ross asked the man to surrender; the warrior replied that he would surrender only when he died. The wounded Comanche then thrust his lance at Ross but missed him. Ross later claimed that he felt pity for the man and refused to kill him. Martinez then told the captain that Nocona and his band had killed his family and made him a slave, and he wanted revenge. Ross then granted Martinez permission to shoot the Comanche. Martinez immediately killed the wounded warrior.[14] Ross gathered some of the man's belongings, leaving some possessions as booty for the other participants in the battle.

Lieutenant Kelliher, meanwhile, disgusted at riding his prized horse so hard after "an old squaw," took the woman and her baby to the camp.[15] The woman continued to weep and Martinez explained that she was Nocona's wife and was crying for her husband and two sons. Upon further investigation, Ross discovered that her eyes were blue and that she was a white woman. Although the woman spoke no English and continued to wail in Comanche, Ross realized that she must be a "captive" and attempted to treat her with kindness.

Before they left the Pease River, the men searched for spoils. Ross later presented Governor Houston with the weapons and personal articles he had taken from the fallen Comanche's body. The Texans captured nearly forty horses and mules, two of which were reclaimed by volunteers from Cureton's company — one horse had been stolen six months earlier and the other had been missing for over two years.

After the captured Indian property had been divided, Ross took the woman and child to Camp Cooper, where another translator questioned her about Peta Nocona and his band. In the process Ross wrote an official report of the battle, and news of the Pease River "victory" quickly spread.

On 2 January 1861 the story was retold in an article in the *Dallas Weekly Herald*. Ross explained that he had found Mrs. Sherman's Bible and Henry Rilly's papers — both Sherman and Rilly had been killed a few months earlier by Nocona's warriors. Ross proclaimed that he had "thrashed them out" with his own party without the help of Captain Cureton's force. He boasted that "all my men acquitted themselves with great honor — proving worthy representatives of true Texas valor," but he failed to point out that the Comanches were mainly women. He added that of his men "not more than 20 were able to get in the fight, owing to the starved and jaded condition of their horses having had no grass after leaving the vicinity of Belknap."[16] Cureton's volunteers angrily responded with complaints that Ross had not waited for them and intentionally left them out of the battle.[17]

One part of the official story to generate controversy was the number of Comanches present at the battle. Figures provided by various accounts varied from fifteen to over five hundred. B. F. Gholson claimed that there were almost six hundred Indians at the Pease River, including approximately two hundred well armed warriors. At the opposite extreme, Ross maintained that there were only fifteen Indians present. Claims of the number of Comanches killed also vary; according to the War Department, fourteen Indians died during the fight. Ross declared that all Comanches in the camp were casualties, with twelve killed and three captured. There were no casualties or wounded among the rangers or regulars, which is not surprising since few warriors seem to have been present.[18]

At Camp Cooper, the captured woman, apparently fearing for her life, refused to answer any questions. Finally, persuaded that the white men meant her no harm, she asked for information concerning her two sons who had been at the camp. The soldiers assured her that since there were no young boys among either the casualties or the captives, they must have escaped. She told Ross through an interpreter that most of the band's warriors had been bartering with Comancheros, or New Mexico traders, exchanging loot acquired during earlier raids for provisions and other commodities.[19] She also explained that prior to the attack, thirty-five warriors had left the camp. The Indians Ross had killed were part of a hunting party — mostly women who had been left there to prepare the meat and disassemble the camp. "I was in the Pease river fight," H. B. Rogers admitted, "but I am not very proud of it. That was not a battle at all, but just a killing of squaws. One or two bucks and sixteen squaws were killed."[20] Other reports also confirmed the fact that the group attacked was a band of women, children, and a few male servants drying meat for winter.[21]

Although Ross was adamant that Peta Nocona was killed at the battle, there were many questions as to whether the chief was even at the Pease River when the rangers arrived. Some people claimed to have seen him years after the attack and rumors circulated that he died in the mid-1870s. The warrior Martinez thought was Nocona, was probably the leader of the hunting party — such a figure usually being referred to as a "chief." Charles Goodnight stated that Ross killed a chief named No-bah, "but Nocona died a long time afterwards while hunting plums on the Canadian."[22] Horace P. Jones stated that he spoke with the chief when the Comanche visited him at Fort Sill in the early 1870s. Quanah Parker's granddaughter, Laura Birdsong, declared that Nocona was away from the camp, but returned after the battle and gathered the remaining Indians, including Cynthia Ann's sons. She asserted that the rangers had killed Joe Nocona, the chief's servant, and that Peta Nocona died several years later from blood poisoning.[23]

Other discrepancies appeared, for there were numerous accounts of the events leading to the identification of the captured white woman. Ross stated that he took her to Mrs. N. G. Evans at Camp Cooper "where she could be properly clothed & cared for." He also reported that he "dispatched a messenger to inform Col Parker, and when he came to my Post, he took along with him my Mexican servant, as an interpreter, he having too been a captive and fully conversant with the Comanche language."[24] According to Goodnight, however, Ross asked Ben Kiggins, a former Comanche captive, to interpret for him.

Horace Jones, the army's interpreter at Camp Cooper in the early 1860s, asserted that he interviewed the woman after the fight. Jones recalled that Capt. Innis N. Palmer summoned him to talk with the woman. Since everyone at Camp Cooper was convinced that she was Cynthia Ann Parker, Palmer asked Jones if he would take her to his house and care for her until she was identified by family or friends. Jones did not like that idea. "I told him I did not wish to take her in charge as she was the same as a wild Indian and would be constantly attempting to make her escape and in all probability succeeding by stealing my horses which were tied in the shed room of my house."[25]

News of the white woman's rescue spread rapidly throughout the area and many inquiries were made about her identity. Still assuming that the woman was Cynthia Ann Parker, officials at Camp Cooper — not Sul Ross — contacted Col. Isaac Parker, her uncle. When Parker arrived at the camp in late January and met with the woman, she claimed neither to know her original name, to understand English, nor to remember where she had come from. According to A. B. Mason, who accompanied Parker to Camp Cooper, the young woman "sat for a time immovable, lost in profound meditation, oblivious to every thing by which she was surrounded, ever and anon convulsed as it were by some powerful emotion which she struggled to suppress."[26] Through Jones, Parker questioned her regarding certain events of her early childhood. When he asked if she remembered her childhood home, she answered that she had resided in a house surrounded by a large clearing, but added that there were plenty of woods within a short distance. The description fit Fort Parker.[27] When Parker questioned her in English she remained silent and appeared unable to understand him. He then turned to Jones and said, "If this is my niece, her name is Cynthia Ann." Before Jones could translate, the woman arose, struck herself on the breast, and exclaimed "Me, Cynthia Ann."[28]

Questioned further by Jones, she recalled the incident at Fort Parker that resulted in her original captivity, but that the only name she remembered was that of her brother John. She dated the raid with surprising accuracy, missing it by only four months. The woman also remembered that she had once had "palefaced parents." There would be no doubt as to her identity — she was thirty-four-year-old Cynthia Ann Parker, a prisoner of the Comanches since the age of nine.

In early February, Mason submitted an article to *The Galveston Civilian* that included a translation of a brief account of her captivity reputedly given by Cynthia Ann at Camp Cooper, but the name of the interpreter was not given. Although some of the narrative's facts are accurate, it is not known how much editing took place to make her story more exciting, articulate, and concise. "I remember when I was a little girl," the report began, "being a long time at a house with a picket fence all around; one day some Indians came to the house, they had a white rag on the stick." Cynthia Ann presumably told the interpreter, "My father [actually her uncle] went out to talk to them, they surrounded and killed him, then many other Indians came and fought at the house; several whites were killed; my mother and her four children were taken prisoners; in the evening mother and two of her children were retaken by a white man." she continued, "My brother died among the Indians of smallpox, I lived with the Indians north of Santa Fe; have three children."[29]

With her recapture, Cynthia Ann was torn from the Indian life to which she had become accustomed. For almost twenty-five years the Comanches had been her people, yet in a brief surprise attack she had been stripped of her husband, her sons, her friends, and ultimately her Indian identity. Her suffering as a result of these losses was apparent in the few remaining years of her life.

Ross's deadly attack on an unarmed camp of women and children temporarily silenced those who charged that the government's policy toward Indians was too lenient. His smashing victory did not end Comanche raids, however, for the attacks intensified during the Civil War. Because the Confederacy needed a steady supply of soldiers, many state units were inducted into the Confederate Army. The demands of the war left few men and little money to maintain the Texas frontier defenses, and the Indians took full advantage of the situation.

During the middle decades of the nineteenth century, violence was endemic on the Texas frontier. Indeed, whites in Texas had been fighting Indians for so many years that most settlers condoned the killing of "savage redmen." In conflicts like the Pease River massacre, anti-Indian hysteria escalated so that women and children were indiscriminately slaughtered. In retrospect the frontier society of Texas that accepted Cynthia Ann's return was no more "civilized" than that of the Comanches.

When Cynthia Ann accompanied her uncle to Birdville, she faced an unstable, hostile environment. She attracted much publicity and was the subject of numerous newspaper articles that focused on her "unfortunate" experiences among the Indians. It is ironic that Texans' fascination with Cynthia Ann centered on the misfortunes they believed she had suffered during captivity among "heathen savages." Actually she seems to have been well treated, for she considered the Comanches her people and was determined to return to them. Yet Cynthia Ann, who obviously would have preferred to remain with her Comanche family, had no choice but to return to her forgotten white relatives.

Almost a quarter of a century had passed since Cynthia Ann's captivity began. With both of her captors claiming the superior culture, Cynthia Ann's conception of her new environment was as skewed as her first impressions of Comanche life must have been. Unless she could return to her adopted people, her hopes for the future must have seemed dismal. No Texan could comprehend that the major tragedy of her life was not being raised as a Comanche, but being snatched from her Comanche husband and sons. Instead, the popular view that she had been saved from a despairing existence among a savage people would eventually help to make Sul Ross — the hero of Pease River — the governor of Texas.

Reluctant Expatriate

Cynthia Ann's reunion with her white family was destined to be unhappy. Her nearly twenty-five years with the Comanches made adjustment almost impossible, for her Indian habits and customs were deeply ingrained. Family and neighbors tried to help her, but their well-intentioned methods only strengthened her desire to return to the Indians. These Texans never understood that Cynthia Ann had been stripped of her Comanche family and was trapped in a strange new environment.

On the condition that her sons would be sent to her if captured, Cynthia Ann agreed to leave Camp Cooper with her uncle in late January 1861. From the camp, Isaac Duke Parker accompanied Cynthia Ann and her daughter to his farm two and a half miles east of Birdville, then the county seat of Tarrant County.[1] They stopped on the way in Fort Worth, where A. F. Corning photographed a grieving Cynthia Ann with her infant daughter at her breast. Her hair was cut short — a Comanche sign of mourning.[2]

Parker then took the newly recovered woman and two-year-old child to his double-log cabin farm house a few miles northeast of Fort

Isaac Parker Cabin. Log Cabin Village, Fort Worth, Texas.
Photograph by Steven Watson.

Worth. Built in the 1850s, his home was considered the finest in the county. The two cabins, joined together by a covered breezeway, was of sufficient size to provide for Cynthia Ann and Topsannah, as well as Isaac Parker's family.[3]

Many changes affected the newcomers upon the arrival at the Parkers' homestead. The family and neighbors immediately demanded that both mother and child forsake their Indian garments for "civilized" clothing. Convinced that Topsannah's soul had been snared by the "demon of barbarianism," they also insisted upon instructing her in biblical scriptures and lessons.[4] Despite the neighbors' attempts to force acculturation upon them, Cynthia Ann resisted, and never stopped grieving for Peta Nocona and her sons, Quanah and Pecos.

In February 1861 a relative of Cynthia Ann, K. J. Pearson, watched as she performed what he termed "her devotions." Pearson indicated that she cleaned a smooth place on the ground and then drew a circle and a cross. She kindled a fire on the cross, burned some tobacco, and then cut her breast to let blood flow onto the flames. Lighting a pipe, she blew smoke toward the sun and meditated. Pearson discovered that this was Cynthia Ann's prayer to "the great spirit to enable her to understand and appreciate" that she was among "relatives and kindred."[5]

Despite such supposed attempts to "understand and appreciate" her white family, Cynthia Ann often attempted to flee with Topsannah to the Comanches. Rumors circulated that her family locked both mother and child inside the double-log cabin every night and at other times when a family member could not watch them.[6] In contrast, Pearson stated that she did not want to return to the Indians because they had often whipped her, and the *Clarksville Northern Standard* reported that her arms and body "bear the marks of having been cruelly treated [by the Comanches]."[7] In the unlikely event that the whites were correct and Cynthia Ann had been mistreated by the Indians, then her prayer to "understand and appreciate" her family might have been genuine. Still she tried to run away. Her family failed to realize that because of the Pease River massacre, Cynthia Ann was again a prisoner who sat for hours on end on the Parkers' front porch with Topsannah at her breast and tears streaming down her face.[8]

A distraught Isaac Parker promised Cynthia Ann that she could visit her Comanche friends if she made an effort to learn English and conform to her new life in white society. Family members and neighbors also renewed their efforts to help her change. In the spring of 1861, Mrs. John Henry Brown, Mrs. Nathaniel C. Raymond, and other family friends took Cynthia Ann to Austin to witness the secession conventions. Preparing her for the trip — which was a social affair — the women dressed her in "neat garments, which she thought very uncomfortable."[9]

On the floor of the House of Representatives, Cynthia Ann became noticeably worried, for she feared that the congressmen were chiefs deliberating on her fate. She tried to run away, but Mrs. Brown restrained her and tried to assure Cynthia Ann that the convention did not concern her and no harm would come her way.[10] While in Austin, Cynthia Ann attracted much attention and numerous people visited her. During her stay she sat again for a photographer; the photo showed a short-haired woman with an uneasy expression upon her face.

At this time, the *Northern Standard* reported that Cynthia Ann originally thought that whites would try to kill her. "She believed that the Comanches were the most numerous and powerful people in the world"; the editors added that "only now was she beginning to learn how much she had been deceived."[11]

After her visit to the state capitol, the Texas Legislature passed an act on 8 April 1861, granting her "a pension of one hundred dollars per annum, for five years . . . to be paid quarterly." The legislature ordered the county court of Tarrant County to appoint a guardian, "who shall give a bond to the Chief Justice of Tarrant County in the sum of five hundred dollars, conditioned for the faithful application of said pension" for her support and for the education of her child.[12] An additional act provided Cynthia Ann with one league of land to be "located, surveyed and patented as other land certificates." Title to the land temporarily rested in Isaac Duke Parker of Tarrant County and Benjamin Parker of Anderson County, who were to hold it in trust after giving "bond and security as required."[13]

Life in Birdville depressed Cynthia Ann. While whites continued to believe that she would "re-assimilate" to her original culture, she constantly feared for her life. Whites viewed Cynthia Ann's life among the Comanches as a "long night of suffering and woe" which could "furnish the material for a tale more interesting than those found in the Arabian Nights Entertainment."[14] Assuming that her years between the ages of nine and thirty-four were full of torture, maltreatment, enslavement, and other brutalities, whites pitied Cynthia Ann and expressed hope that, as one newspaper stated, her latter years of "earthly existence [spent with white people]" would be more pleasant than those of her life with the "savage redmen."[15]

Life at her uncle's house remained unpleasant for Cynthia Ann, and ultimately Isaac Parker asked her younger brother, Silas M. Parker, Jr., if she and her child could live with him. In the years after he and Lucy Parker had escaped from the Indians during the raid on Fort Parker in 1836, Silas had married and established a farm north of Tyler in Van Zandt County.[16] He agreed to house Cynthia Ann and Topsannah and they moved there in late 1861. Early in the following year, the Texas Legislature appointed Silas Parker as her new guardian.[17]

Cynthia Ann's experience at her brother's home was equally depressing. Again her family promised Cynthia Ann and Topsannah that they could return to the Comanche camps to visit friends and possibly locate her sons Quanah and Pecos. The Civil War, however, postponed her reunion. A Union blockade soon restricted supplies to East Texas and many men left the settlements to join the war. The women were forced to manage the farms and businesses as well as perform daily household tasks and care of their families. These women needed as much help as possible, and Cynthia Ann was expected to participate. She apparently complied and reportedly learned new techniques of spinning, weaving, and sewing.

Although her tannery skills impressed the Van Zandt women, the relationship between Cynthia Ann and her sister-in-law Mary deteriorated. Silas's wife never adjusted to the presence of Cynthia Ann and the Indian child in her home. She punished Topsannah every time she referred to her mother as Preloch — Cynthia Ann's Comanche name — or pretended she was an Indian "princess."[18] Topsannah became known as "Little Barbarian" shortly after arriving in Van Zandt County.

Cynthia Ann later moved with Topsannah to her sister Orlena's house near Slater's Creek, where her brother-in-law, Ruff O'Quinn owned a farm. There she met T. J. Cates of Ben Wheeler, Texas, who remembered Cynthia Ann as

> stout and weighed about 140 pounds, well-made, and liked to work. She had a wild expression and would look down when people looked at her. She could use an ax equal to a man and disliked a lazy person. She was an expert in tanning hides with the hair on them, or plaiting or knitting either ropes or whips. She thought her two boys were lost on the prairie . . . this dissatisfied her very much.

Every Sunday, Cates and his wife took Topsannah, whom they called "Tecks Ann," visiting.[19] This "pretty and sprightly" child quickly learned English, and neighbors commented proudly that she spoke it more often than Comanche. But tragically in the fall of 1863, the young child suddenly contracted a fever which developed into influenza and pneumonia. The five-year-old Topsannah died on 15 December 1863.[20] Her grief-stricken mother and other relatives quietly buried Topsannah in Asbury graveyard, eight miles south of Ben Wheeler.

Topsannah's death devastated Cynthia Ann. Heartbroken, she agreed to move to a small sawmill that the O'Quinns owned near the county line of Henderson and Anderson counties. She stayed there for the remaining years of her life. In 1870, weakened by self-inflicted starvation, Cynthia Ann contracted "la grippe" (influenza) and died.[21]

Joe and Bob Paggitt built Cynthia Ann's coffin and arranged the simple funeral. Joe's wife prepared her for burial and placed a bone pin in her hair; they buried her in the Foster Cemetery, four miles south of Poyner near the Anderson-Henderson County line.[22]

Cynthia Ann's story does not end with her death. Her family continued to share the history of the Texas-Oklahoma frontier. Unlike other Comanche warriors who married several times during their lifetime, Peta Nocona never took another wife. Learning of the attack when he returned to the campsite on the Pease River, he took his sons and retreated into Oklahoma. Unsure of what had occurred at the camp, Nocona had difficulty gathering information about the attack since all of the Indians present had been either killed or captured.[23]

Almost two years after the massacre, Nocona learned that Camp Cooper's interpreter, Horace Jones, had been transferred to Fort Cobb on the Washita River, north of Fort Sill. Nocona arranged a meeting with Jones and after the two smoked a pipe, the Comanche told the interpreter that he wanted only to hear the truth about Cynthia Ann. Recounting the story of her capture and Isaac Parker's identification of her, Jones explained that he never saw her again after she left for East Texas. He remembered Cynthia Ann's concern for her sons, and he asked about their welfare. Nocona replied that they were far away on the prairie "where you cannot see them, but some day you may."[24] Jones never saw Peta Nocona again, yet throughout the decade rumors periodically reached posts in Texas and Oklahoma that the Comanche was hunting in the Panhandle. He evidently died in the middle 1870s. Shortly after Peta Nocona's meeting with Jones, Cynthia Ann's son, Pecos, fell victim to smallpox.[25]

The other son, Quanah, survived his parents, grew to manhood, and eventually became one of the most sagacious Comanche chiefs. Born during the early 1840s, Quanah was almost twenty at the time of his mother's capture. He became a warrior and by the mid-1860s joined the Quahada band of Comanches. Whites feared these Indians whom they called the most "wild and hostile" of all the tribesmen. During all their forays, however, Quanah reportedly never allowed his followers to kill any white women or children. He told several families that since his mother and sister were living with white people somewhere, he wished to avoid the possibility of their being accidentally harmed.[26]

The Quahadas' reputation peaked after they defeated Col. Ranald S. Mackenzie and the Fourth Calvary at Blanco Canyon in October

Quanah Parker. Joseph E. Taulman Collection,
Barker Texas History Center, The University of Texas at Austin.

1871. Only three years later, however, the last of the Comanche raids took place, and after their defeat at the Battle of Adobe Walls, the Quahadas retreated into the Blanco Canyon region.

With the buffalo rapidly disappearing and soldiers increasing on the frontier, more Indians were forced onto reservations. By April 1875 Quanah also agreed to surrender; within weeks one hundred Quahada warriors, three hundred women and children, and fourteen hundred horses arrived at Fort Sill, marking an end to their nomadic existence.

Upon arrival at the fort, Quanah immediately made inquiries about his mother, hoping to be united with her. In a letter to Col. E. J. Strange in Denison, Mackenzie (by then Quanah's friend) wrote, "a Qua-ha-de Comanche, who came into this post a few days ago, is the son of . . . Cynthia Ann Parker." Quanah, the general explained, was "very desirous of finding out the whereabouts of his mother, if still alive." The letter was passed on to many people until it reached Maj. John Henry Brown of Dallas. Brown replied through a published article in the *Dallas Weekly Herald*, furnishing the "wild and unknown kinsman" with names of Cynthia Ann's relatives."[27] In response to the newspaper report, Mackenzie learned that Cynthia Ann had died almost five years earlier, and he informed Quanah of the sad news.

On 5 September 1877 Mackenzie wrote Isaac Parker at Quanah's request. Planning a trip to East Texas, the Comanche wanted to make sure his white relatives would welcome him into their home. Mackenzie noted that Quanah was "a man whom it is worth trying to do something with," and that he "certainly should not be held responsible for the sins of a former generation of comanches [sic]." Quanah and Mackenzie, however, did not receive a response from the Parker family.

A few years later Quanah advertised in various newspapers asking for a picture of his mother. A. F. Corning responded to this request and sent him a copy of the photograph taken over twenty years earlier.[29] With the photo in hand, Quanah desired to learn more about his mother and her capture by the rangers. Agent P. Hunt of the Kiowa, Comanche, and Wichita Agency assisted him by writing letters to various Parker relatives.[30] By 1880 Quanah had learned of the pension and land the Texas Legislature had granted his mother in 1861. Hunt tried to hire a lawyer on Quanah's behalf to locate any inheritance to which he might be entitled, although no counsel, money, or land were even obtained.[31]

In 1907, Quanah wrote Texas governor Thomas Campbell. "Well Mr. Governor, my mother Cynthia Ann Parker was captured by Governor Ross," he explained. At that time, he continued, the Texas legislature "gave her 160 acres of land and g[a]ve her $500.00 a year to help the poor woman."[32] Quanah stated that his mother never received the land or the money and he asked the governor to assist him in obtaining them.[33]

Meanwhile, Quanah attempted to locate his mother's grave, pursuant to bringing her remains to Oklahoma. In November 1910, after much investigation, Aubrey Birdsong, Quanah's son-in-law, found Cynthia Ann's gravesite near Poyner, Texas. The U. S. Congress granted Quanah $800 to finance his mother's reburial at Post Oak Mission cemetery, five miles from Quanah's home in Cache, Oklahoma, and on 4 December the service was held. After two sermons and two songs, in both Comanche and English, Quanah addressed the large crowd, recounting how Cynthia Ann had been captured by the Indians. His mother, Quanah proclaimed, loved her life among the Comanches so much that she never wanted to return to her white family. He added, however, that they were "all same people, anyway." Quanah stood "in tears and deep agony" throughout the remainder of the funeral.[34]

Still concerned with the land promised to Cynthia Ann by the Texas government, Quanah wrote Charles Goodnight a month after her remains had been taken to Oklahoma. "Mr. Charlie I want you to help me with my [mother's] property. I want you to write to your representative at Austin and tell him to look the matter up." He explained that he had written to others about the land, but the problem had not been resolved. The aged Quanah stated he was eager for a quick and final resolution to the land question and he needed Goodnight's immediate assistance.[35]

Quanah lived only one month longer. Developing pneumonia in mid-February 1911, he died on the twenty-third and was buried next to his mother. The land, however, was never located nor did Cynthia Ann or any of her relatives ever receive the pension.

In 1957, the U. S. government ordered the removal of Cynthia Ann, Quanah, and seven hundred other Comanches buried at the Post Oak Mission so that the military could build proving grounds for guided missiles. Maj. Gen. Thomas E. deShazo supervised the transfer of Cynthia Ann's and Quanah's remains to the military cemetery at Fort Sill. Because of Quanah's leadership among the Comanches, both services were performed "with due military ceremony" on 9 August 1957. In 1965 Topsannah's remains were also brought to Fort Sill.[36]

Cynthia Ann's story has been the topic of both legends and folklore ever since her capture a century and a half earlier. Narratives of her life are still being written emphasizing the tragic circumstances she had to endure among both the Comanches and the whites. At the age of nine, she had witnessed the death of her father and other relatives and was abducted, never to see her mother again. After she was returned to the whites, she became another captive — losing her husband, children, and ultimately, her identity as an Indian. When Topsannah died in 1863, Cynthia Ann had nothing left of her Comanche life other than memories.

Her descendants claim that Cynthia Ann died "broken in spirit, a mis-fit among the white people, and bitter at her enforced captivity."[37] Her acquiescence to the wishes of her family had thrust her into a foreign environment where, without her husband or children, she languished only a few years. Her only solace had been the promise that when the Civil War ended she could visit her Indian family. But that hope proved insufficient to sustain her after the loss of her daughter, and she died still a Comanche in her heart and mind.

CONCLUSION

From childhood until death, Cynthia Ann's destiny was often beyond her control. In the course of her life she suffered the loss of parents, husband, children, and ultimately even her identity. To the Indians she was the respected wife of war chief Peta Nocona. To whites she was a poignant victim of frontier strife, a tragic misfit unable to appreciate her good fortune when rescued from a degrading life among savages. Her legacy was perhaps greater than they ever imagined, for her son Quanah Parker emerged as the most influential Comanche of the reservation era. Through his leadership, peace and friendship between Comanches and whites became a reality after more than a century of hatred and war.

Throughout the nineteenth and twentieth centuries, Cynthia Ann's experiences have been recounted in many histories, folktales, legends, and narratives as well as numerous other forms of hearsay. Today her tale is also heard in operas, plays, motion pictures, and even on the radio. Cynthia Ann's life has generated so much fiction and speculation that it is difficult to determine the truth about her Comanche experiences.

While all of these accounts relate different versions of Cynthia Ann's experiences, it is obvious that she was an incredibly lonely woman from December 1860 until her death. Uprooted from the life and family she loved and trapped in a new environment, Cynthia Ann was forced to settle down and adapt to the unfamiliar ways of white society. Confined to a cabin, she pined for the free and nomadic existence she had known in a Comanche tipi.

Torn from her Indian family and friends, Cynthia Ann had to adjust to a life she had known for only nine years and long ago forgotten. She had been young enough to assimilate so completely to Indian life that she had become thoroughly Comanche. In December 1860, almost twenty-five years after the Fort Parker incident, it was impossible for Cynthia Ann to re-assimilate.

For decades no white Texan could comprehend the real tragedy of Cynthia Ann Parker's life. Although whites believed that the "disgrace" of being a Comanche warrior's "squaw" was her greatest misfortune, the major catastrophe was not her capture and existence among Comanches, but her separation from her Indian husband and sons and the way of life to which she had become attached. Paradoxically, the popular view that she had been "rescued" from a degrading existence among "savages" prevailed over the heartbreaking loss of husband and sons.

NOTES

CHAPTER ONE

1. Grace Jackson, *Cynthia Ann Parker* (San Antonio: Naylor Co., 1959), 1-5. Unfortunately there are no Federal Population Censuses for Georgia in 1790 and 1800, nor for Bedford County, Tennessee, in 1810.

2. Other sources state Coles and Crawford Counties instead of Clark County, see James T. DeShields, *Border Wars of Texas* (Tioga, Texas: Herald Co., 1912), 173, and Jackson, *Cynthia Ann Parker*, 5. There are, however, several Parkers including, Silas, John, Benjamin, Nathaniel, and Isaac, on the 1830 Federal Population Census for Clark County, Illinois. Daniel Parker is listed on the 1830 Census for Crawford County. 1830 Federal Population Census, Clark County, Illinois, Records of the Bureau of the Census, National Archives Microfilm Publication M19, roll 23.

3. Jackson, *Cynthia Ann Parker*, 6.

4. Margaret Waldraven-Johnson, *White Comanche: The Story of Cynthia Ann Parker and her Son, Quanah* (New York: Comet, 1956), 1.

5. Mamie Folsom Wynne, "History Centers About Cynthia Ann Parker's Home," in *Women Tell the Story of the Southwest*, Mattie L. Wooten, ed. (San Antonio: Naylor Co., 1940), 121; Gene Fallwell, *The Comanche Trail of Thunder and the Massacre at Parker's Fort* (Dallas: Highlands Historical Press, 1958), 5.

6. Jackson, *Cynthia Ann Parker*, 10; J. B. Parker, personal interview, 14 May 1985. This second group consisted primarily of members of the "Pilgrim Predestinarian Regular Baptist Church" which Daniel Parker established in 1833 while ignoring Mexican law. His church has been reconstructed and each year Parker family members in Elkhart perform a pageant depicting the early days of the settlement. Daniel was one of the signers of the Declaration of Independence for Texas in 1836. He died in Anderson County in 1845.

7. Fort Houston consisted of a store and half a dozen cabins within the fortification. From 1836-1839, this fort was important for white settlers' security. It was abandoned in 1841.

8. Jackson, *Cynthia Ann Parker*, 15.

9. Frank Brown, "Annals of Travis County and the City of Austin (From the Earliest Times to the Close of 1875)," chap. 21, Frank Brown Papers, Eugene C. Barker Texas History Center, University of Texas, Austin, 32.

10. Silas M. Parker to the General Council of Texas, 2 November 1835, Old Fort Parker State Historical Site, Groesbeck, Texas.

11. Albert Bigelow Paine, *Captain Bill McDonald: Texas Ranger* (New York: J. J. Little and Ives, 1909), 127; Notes by Daniel Parker, 18 June 1836, Parker Documents, Eugene C. Barker Texas History Center, University of Texas.

12. Accounts range from 500 to 700 Indians surrounding the fort.

13. Rachel Plummer, *Rachel Plummer's Narrative of 21 Months Servitude As a Prisoner Among the Comanche Indians* (Houston: Telegraph Power Press, 1838; repr., Austin: Jenkins Publishing Co., 1977), 2. This highly emotional account was drafted less than a year after Plummer's release from the Comanches. Unfortunately there is not a recorded Indian version of the Fort Parker attack to provide some balance to the her narrative.

14. Fallwell, *The Comanche Trail*, 10.

15. Plummer, *Rachel Plummer's Narrative of 21 Months*, 6.

16. Ibid.

17. William Henry Jackson, "Interesting Accounts of Early Day Events as Recounted by Member of a Pioneer Limestone County Family," *The Groesbeck Journal* (Texas), 15 May 1936, sec. 3, 4.

18. Rachel Plummer, *The Rachel Plummer Narrative* (Louisville, Ky.: Morning Courier Office, 1844; repr., Palestine, Tex.: 1926), 9. This narrative is the second edition to *Rachel Plumme* *arrative of 21 Months*; the preface is dated 1839, but the book was not actually published until 1844, and then only as an appendix to James W. Parker's own story about the Fort Parker raid, *Narrative of the Perilous Adventures, Miraculous Escapes and Sufferings of Rev. James W. Parker. . .to which is appended a Narrative of the Capture and Subsequent Sufferings of Mrs. Rachel Plummer.*

19. Ibid., 11.

CHAPTER TWO

1. Rachel Plummer, *Rachel Plummer's Narrative of 21 Months Servitude as a Prisoner among the Comanche Indians* (Houston: Telegraph Press, 1838; repr., Austin: Jenkins, 1977), 7.

2. Paul I. Wellman, *Glory, God and Gold* (New York: Doubleday & Co., 1954), 248.

3. Rachel Plummer, *The Rachel Plummer Narrative* (Louisville, Ky.: Morning Courier Office, 1844; repr., Palestine, Tex.: 1926), 14-15.

4. Plummer, *Rachel Plummer's Narrative of 21 Months Servitude*, 11.

5. Plummer, *The Rachel Plummer Narrative*, 98.

6. *A Memorial and Biographical History of Navarro, Henderson, Anderson, Limestone, Freestone, and Leon Counties, Texas* (Chicago: Lewis Publishing Co., 1893), 329.

7. Plummer, *Rachel Plummer's Narrative of 21 Months Servitude*, 11.

8. Donohue ransomed several white captives during his life. In 1837 he ransomed a Mrs. Harris and a Mrs. Horn from Comanches. John Henry Brown, *Indian Wars and Pioneers of Texas* (Austin: L. E. Daniell, 1880), 36.

9. *Houston Telegraph and Texas Register*, 27 July 1842, 1.

10. Frank X. Tolbert, *An Informal History of Texas* (New York: Harper and Brothers, 1961), 124. A James P. Plumer is listed on the 1850 Federal Population Census for Houston County, and a J. P. Plummer is included on the 1860 census for the same

county. 1850 Federal Population Census, Houston County, Texas, Records of the Bureau of the Census, National Archives Microfilm Publication M432, roll 911; 1860 Federal Population Census, Houston County, Texas, National Archives Microfilm Publication M653, roll 1297.

11. Sam Houston to William Henry Daingerfield, 10 December 1842. Sam Houston, *The Writings of Sam Houston, 1813-1863*, ed. Amelia W. Williams and Eugene C. Barker (Austin: University of Texas Press, 1938-43), 2:231.

12. See James T. DeShields, *Cynthia Ann Parker: The Story of Her Capture* (St. Louis: 1886; repr., New York: Garland, 1976); J. Frank Dobie, *On the Open Range* (Dallas: Southwest Press, 1931); *A Memorial and Biographical History of Navarro. . .*; Margaret Waldraven-Johnson, *White Comanche: The Story of Cynthia Ann Parker and her Son, Quanah* (New York: Comet, 1956); Paul I. Wellman, "Cynthia Ann Parker," *Chronicles of Oklahoma*, 12 (no. 2, 1934): 163-71.

13. Charles Adams Gulick, Jr., ed. *The Papers of Mirabeau Buonaparte Lamar* (Austin: Von Boeckmann-Jones Co., 1924), no. 2166.

14. Earl Henry Elam, "The Butler and Lewis Mission and Treaty of 1846," *West Texas Historical Association Yearbook*, 46 (1970): 90.

15. Paul I. Wellman, "Cynthia Ann Parker," *Chronicles of Oklahoma*, vol. 12, no. 2 (1934): 163.

16. "Report of Messrs. Butler and Lewis," House of Representatives, War Department, Document No. 76, 29th Cong., 2d sess., 8.

17. Ibid.

18. Wellman, "Cynthia Ann Parker," 126; H. G. Bedford, *Texas Indian Troubles* (Dallas: Hargreaves Printing Co., 1905), 60.

19. Randolph Barnes Marcy, *Thirty Years of Army Life on the Border* (New York: Harper & Brothers, 1866), 55.

20. Letter to the Editor, *Washington-on-the-Brazos Texas National Register*, 26 June 1845, 7.

21. Ibid.

22. *Houston Telegraph and Texas Register*, 1 June 1846.

23. Neighbors to Medill, 18 November 1847, in Kenneth Franklin Neighbours, *Robert Simpson Neighbors and the Texas Frontier 1836-1859* (Waco: Texian Press, 1975), 41. See also Rupert N. Richardson, *The Comanche Barrier to the South Plains Settlement* (Glendale, Calif.: Arthur H. Clark Co., 1933), 91.

24. DeShields, *Cynthia Ann Parker: The Story of Her Capture*, 32.

25. Wellman, "Cynthia Ann Parker," 164.

CHAPTER THREE

1. Lamar passed a series of acts designed to provide white settlers who lived on the frontier with protection against certain bands of Comanches and other tribes. He also accepted the services of "Mounted Volunteers" for the "Ranging Service." See *Laws of Texas, 1822-1897*, vol. 2, 15- 16, 29-30, 84-85.

2. See Kenneth Franklin Neighbours, *Robert Simpson Neighbors and the Texas Frontier, 1836-1859* (Waco: The Texian Press, 1975), 29; W. W. Newcomb, Jr., *The Indians of Texas* (Austin: University of Texas Press, 1978), 350; and Walter Prescott Webb, *The Texas Rangers* (Austin: University of Texas Press, 1965), 55. For the federal government's

version of the Council House Massacre, see the *Journals of the House of Representatives of the Republic of Texas*, 5th Cong., 1st sess., appendix, 133ff.

3. Fort Belknap, founded during the summer of 1851, was named for Gen. William Goldsmith Belknap. The soldiers abandoned the fort in 1859 since it lacked an adequate water supply and moved to Camp Cooper. Barbara A. Neal Ledbetter, *Fort Belknap, Frontier Saga* (Burnet, Tex.: Eakin Press, 1982), 89.

4. See Kenneth F. Neighbours, "Fort Belknap," in *Frontier Forts of Texas* (Waco: Texian Press, 1966), 5-19.

5. T. R. Fehrenbach, *Comanches* (New York: Alfred A. Knopf, 1979), 436.

6. Neighbours, *Robert Simpson Neighbors*, 227. Rip Ford refused orders from the governor and a judge to arrest the murderers of Choctaw Tom's group. Ford argued that he was a military man and not a police officer. Bern Keating, *An Illustrated History of the Texas Rangers* (Chicago: Rand McNally & Co., 1975), 80.

7. Elizabeth Ross Clarke, "YA-A-H-HOO, Warwhoop of the Comanches, the Cry that Struck Terror to the Hearts of the Pioneers in the Early Days of Texas," n.d., Elizabeth R. Clarke Papers, Eugene C. Barker Texas History Center, University of Texas, Austin, Tex.

8. H. G. Bedford, *Texas Indian Troubles* (Dallas: Hargreaves Printing Co., 1905), 71.

9. Buckley B. Paddock, ed., *A Twentieth Century History and Biographical Record of North and West Texas*, (New York: Lewis Publishing Co., 1906), 1: 92-93.

10. *The Galveston Civilian*, 15 January 1861.

11. Many rangers wrote narratives; however, some were written decades after the Pease River fight.

12. *The Galveston Civilian*, 15 January 1861.

13. Rupert N. Richardson, "The Death of Nocona and the Recovery of Cynthia Ann Parker," *Southwest Historical Quarterly*, 46 (July 1942): 16.

14. Judith Ann Benner, *Sul Ross: Soldier, Statesman, Educator* (College Station: Texas A & M University Press, 1983), 54.

15. J. P. Earl, "Quanah and Cynthia Ann Parker," chap. 18 of "J. P. Earl Narrative," Eugene C. Barker Texas History Center, University of Texas, Austin.

16. *Dallas Weekly Herald*, 2 January 1861; *The Galveston Civilian*, 15 January 1861.

17. Judith Ann Benner, "Lone Star Soldier: A Study of the Military Career of Lawrence Sullivan Ross" (Ph. D. diss. Texas Christian University, 1975), 118.

18. *Dallas Herald*, 2 January 1861; Adjutant General's Office, *Chronological List of Actions, &c., With Indians from January 15, 1837 to January 1891*, (Fort Collins, Colo.: Old Army Press, 1979), 22.

19. *The Galveston Civilian*, 15 January 1861.

20. B. F. Gholson, "B. F. Gholson Recollections," B. F. Gholson Papers, Eugene C. Barker Texas History Center, 70.

21. Interview with Laura Birdsong by Robert B. Thomas, September 1937, *Indian-Pioneer Papers*, WPA Project, Western History Collection, University of Oklahoma, 180. Hereinafter cited as Birdsong Interview.

22. J. Evetts Haley, *Charles Goodnight: Cowman and Plainsman* (Norman: University of Oklahoma Press, 1949), 57.

23. Birdsong Interview; *Marion T. Brown, Marion T. Brown: Letters from Fort Sill, 1886-1887*, ed. C. Richard King (Austin: Encino Press, 1970), 78.

24. Ross to Victor M. Rose, 5 October 1880, Ross Papers, Texas Collection, Baylor University (copy from Robertson Colony Collection, University of Texas at Arlington).

25. Brown, *Marion T. Brown: Letters from Fort Sill*, 78.

26. *The Galveston Civilian*, 5 February 1861.
27. Brown, *Marion T. Brown: Letters from Fort Sill*, 78.
28. *The Galveston Civilian*, 5 February 1861.
29. Ibid.

CHAPTER FOUR

1. Birdville was located near present day Haltom City. In the late nineteenth century, a fire broke out in the town's courthouse, destroying most of the early documents.

2. Elizabeth Ross Clarke, "YA-A-H-HOO, Warwhoop of the Comanches, the Cry that Struck Terror to the Hearts of the Pioneers in the Early Days of Texas," n.d., Elizabeth R. Clarke Papers, Eugene C. Barker Texas History Center, University of Texas, Austin, 70 (hereafter cited as Clarke, "YA-A-H-HOO"); Adolph F. Bandelier, *Southwestern Journals of Adolph F. Bandelier*, ed. Charles H. Lange and Carroll L. Riley (Albuquerque: University of New Mexico Press, 1966), 102.

3. John A. Graves and Fred R. Cotten, *Home Place* (N.p.: Pioneer Texas Heritage Committee, 1958); Don Williams, "Visitor Recalls How Log Cabin In Park Looked In Later Years," *Fort Worth Star-Telegram*, 31 January 1960, 8. Amon G. Carter purchased the Parker house in the 1920s and removed it to his country estate, "Shady Oaks," on Lake Worth. In 1959 it was moved to a historical log cabin village in Fort Worth. Mamie Folsom Wynne, "History Centers About Cynthia Ann Parker's Home," in Mattie L. Wooten, ed. *Women Tell the Story of the Southwest* (San Antonio: Naylor Publishing, 1940), 120.

4. Jan Isbelle Fortune, "The Recapture and Return of Cynthia Ann Parker," *The Groesbeck Journal* (Texas), 15 May 1936, 1.

5. K. J. Pearson to John D. Floyd, 3 February 1861, Quanah Parker Files, Fort Sill Archives. Pearson married one of Cynthia Ann's relatives and lived near Fort Worth when she lived with Isaac Parker. T. J. Cates described the same ceremony when Cynthia Ann lived with her sister near Ben Wheeler, Texas. He explained, however, that she performed it in mourning. Paul I. Wellman, "Cynthia Ann Parker," *Chronicles of Oklahoma*, 12(no. 2, 1934): 169.

6. Frank X. Tolbert, "This Cabin Was Cynthia Ann's Jail," *Dallas Morning News*, 12 March 1959, sec. 4, 3; Tolbert, *An Informal History of Texas* (New York: Harper & Brothers, 1961), 135.

7. *Clarksville Northern Standard* (Texas), 6 April 1861, 2. Cynthia Ann could have received these markings during the Pease River Massacre or while performing the strenuous daily work of Comanche women.

8. Although no narratives describe a specific runaway attempt, most sources admit that Cynthia Ann frequently tried to escape back to the Indians. Pauline Durrett Robertson and R. L. Robertson, *Panhandle Pilgrimage* (Amarillo: Paramount Publishing Co., 1978), 72.

9. Mary M. Brown, *A Condensed History of Texas for Schools. . .* (Dallas: 1895), 198.

10. Wynne, "History Centers About Cynthia Ann Parker's Home," 122.

11. *Clarksville Northern Standard*.

12. *The Laws of Texas*, 1822-1897, 10 Volumes (Austin: The Gammel Book Co., 1898), 5: 423-24.

13. Ibid., 5: 426.

14. *Dallas Herald*, 14 April 1861, 1.

15. Ibid.

16. The fate of Cynthia Ann's mother, Lucy Parker, is a mystery. Most accounts claim that she died soon after the raid in 1836. Other reports state that she married a man named Usury some years after the attack. Quanah Parker Files, Fort Sill Archives.

17. *The Laws of Texas*, 5: 556.

18. Fortune, "The Recapture and Return of Cynthia Ann Parker."

19. Grace Jackson, *Cynthia Ann Parker* (San Antonio: Naylor Co., 1959), 98.

20. Frank X. Tolbert questions whether Topsannah actually died or was taken from Cynthia Ann at this time. *Informal Texas History*, 135. William Boas McAlpin claimed to be Topsannah's son. He stated that she returned to the Comanches after Cynthia Ann's death. Interview with William Boas McAlpin by Nannie Lee Burns, 3 January 1938, *Indian-Pioneer Papers*, 57: 21, WPA Project, Western History Collection, University of Oklahoma.

21. In the past there has been controversy over the date of Cynthia Ann's death. Many sources stated that she died in 1864; at Fort Parker her memorial is inscribed with that date. The actual date of her death is several years later. Cynthia Ann Parker is included in the 1870 Federal Population Census. She is listed as a forty-five-year-old housekeeper, born in Illinois. We can confirm her as being the Cynthia Ann Parker in question because the Census indicates that she was currently living with her sister Orlena O'Quinn, near Palestine, Texas. Although the date of her death is as yet unconfirmed, she lived at least until 1870. There is no known obituary notice, but an 1875 *Dallas Weekly Herald* article cited the date of her death as 1870 and her grave-stone in Oklahoma is also marked with an 1870 date. She probably died between June and December 1870 because she was not listed on the 1870 Texas Mortality Schedule which was compiled after 1 June. 1870 Federal Population Census, Anderson County, Texas, Records of the Bureau of the Census, National Archives Microfilm Publication M593, roll 1573, p. 212, line 19; *Dallas Weekly Herald*, 5 June 1875. See also John Henry Brown, *Indian Wars and Pioneers of Texas* (Austin: L. E. Daniell, 1880), 43.

Sources using the 1864 date include James T. DeShields, *Cynthia Ann Parker: The Story of her Capture* (St. Louis: 1886), 72; Carl Coke Rister, *Border Captives: the Traffic in Prisoners by Southern Plains Indians, 1835-1875* (Norman: University of Oklahoma Press, 1940), 83; and Grace Jackson, *Cynthia Ann Parker*, 97. One source used both dates: Malcolm D. McLean, ed., *Papers Concerning Robertson's Colony in Texas, Vol. 14*. McLean, on page 74 of his narrative, states that she died in 1864, but the caption under her photograph on page 87 reads 1870. Still some sources use 1865 or 1871 as the date of her death. See J. P. Earl Narrative, chap. 18, Eugene C. Barker Historical Center, Austin, 70-82, and Jack Selden, "On the Trail of Cynthia Ann Parker," *Texas Highways*, vol. 30, no. 10, October 1983, 36-41.

22. Aubrey Birdsong, Sworn Affidavit, 2 September 1956. Quanah Parker Files, Fort Sill Archives. Starting in 1964, Eugene O'Quinn wrote to various people who might have known his great aunt, Cynthia Ann. He asked questions concerning the date of her death, which he believed to be 1864, and asked whether her daughter Topsannah had been buried with her. Annie Milner to Eugene O'Quinn, 23 October 1964; Annie and John Milner to Eugene O'Quinn, 13 November 1964; Eugene O'Quinn to Sam Pagitt, 24 November 1964; Sam Pagitt to Eugene O'Quinn, 30 November 1964; Elma Scarborough to Eugene O'Quinn, 30 November 1964; Virginia Murphey to Eugene O'Quinn, 13 December 1964; Quanah Parker Files, Fort Sill Archives.

23. Prospective contacts at Camp Cooper who could describe the massacre to Peta Nocona were transferred to various posts after the camp was abandoned in 1861. Wellman, "Cynthia Ann Parker," 169.

24. Marion T. Brown, *Marion T. Brown: Letters from Fort Sill, 1886-1887*, ed. C. Richard King (Austin: Encino Press, 1970), 79-80.

25. George W. Winningham of the *Groesbeck Journal* (Texas) doubts the existence of Pecos. He states that Quanah never mentioned any brother, "if such a child was born to Cynthia Ann, he died in infancy, and Indians do not count them as members of their family." George W. Winningham, "Cynthia Ann Parker," *The Fredricksburg Radio Post* (Texas), 24 December 1964.

26. Angie Debo, "Two Graves in Oklahoma," *Harper's Magazine*, 213 (December 1956): 65.

27. Letter to the Editor, *Dallas Weekly Herald*, 5 June 1875, 1; *Denison Daily Cresset*, 24 May 1875, 4.

28. William T. Hagan, *United Sates-Comanche Relations: The Reservation Years* (New Haven: Yale University Press, 1976), 155.

29. Elizabeth Ross Clarke, "YA-A-H-HOO," 70, 73; James T. DeShields, *Cynthia Ann Parker, The Story of Her Capture* (St. Louis: 1886; repr., New York: Garland, 1976), v; Hagan, *United States-Comanche Relations*, 155.

30. P. A. Hunt to Benjamin Parker, 4 September 1875, Miscellaneous Files, Oklahoma Historical Society, Oklahoma City.

31. P. A. Hunt to H. O. Head, 2 July 1880, Miscellaneous Files, Oklahoma Historical Society.

32. Obviously Quanah was wrong about the amount of money in the pension. Quanah Parker to Gov. Thomas Campbell, 25 November 1907. James M. Day, "Two Quanah Parker Letters," *Chronicles of Oklahoma*, 44 (Autumn 1966): 313-18.

33. Ibid., 316.

34. Neda Parker Birdsong to J. Pagitte, 8 December 1910, Quanah Parker Files, Fort Sill Archives; Aubrey Birdsong, Sworn Affidavit, 2 September 1956, Quanah Parker Files, Fort Sill Archives.

35. Quanah Parker to Charles Goodnight, 7 January 1911, Quanah Parker Files, Fort Sill Archives.

36. J. Nelson Taylor, "Chief's Remains Stir Trouble," *Oklahoma City Daily Oklahoman*, 26 June 1957, Quanah Parker Files, Fort Sill Archives; T. E. deShazo to Joe Bailey Parker, 30 July 1957, copy in possession of author.

38. Wellman, 169.

BIBLIOGRAPHY

Primary Sources

Manuscript Collections

Arlington, Texas. University of Texas at Arlington.
Robertson Colony Collection.
Austin, Texas. University of Texas. Eugene C. Barker
   History Center.
   Frank Brown Papers
   Elizabeth Ross Clarke Papers
   J. P. Earl Narrative
   B. F. Gholson Papers
   Baldwin Parker Papers
   Parker Family Documents.
   Joseph E. Taulman Collection
Fort Worth, Texas. National Archives-Southwest Region.
   Federal Population Censuses 1830 -1870.
Groesbeck, Texas. Old Fort Parker State Historical Site.
   Silas M. Parker to the General Council of Texas, 2 November 1835.
Lawton, Oklahoma. Fort Sill Archives. Quanah Parker Files.
Norman, Oklahoma. Western History Collections. University of Oklahoma Library.
   Indian-Pioneer Papers.
Oklahoma City, Oklahoma. Oklahoma Historical Society.
   Miscellaneous Files.

Interviews

J. P. Parker, Interview with author, 14 May 1985.

Books

Adjutant General's Office. *Chronological List of Actions, &c., With Indians from January 15, 1837 to January 1891.* Fort Collins, Colorado: Old Army Press, 1979.

Brown, Marion T. *Marion T. Brown: Letters from Fort Sill, 1886-1887*. Edited by C. Richard King. Austin: Encino Press, 1970.

Journals of the House of Representatives of the Republic of Texas. 5th Congress, 1st Session.

Report of Messrs. Butler and Lewis. House of Representatives, War Department, Document No. 70. 29th Congress, 2nd Session.

Articles

Day, James M. "Two Quanah Parker Letters," *Chronicles of Oklahoma*. 44 (Autumn, 1966): 313-18.

Newspapers

Clarksville Northern Standard (Texas). 6 April 1861.

Dallas Weekly Herald. 2 January 1861, 17 April 1861, 5 June 1875, 19 June 1875.

Dallas Morning News. 12 March 1959.

Denison Daily Cresset (Texas). 24 May 1875.

Fort Worth Star-Telegram. 31 January 1960.

The Fredricksburg Radio Post (Texas). 24 December 1864.

The Galveston Civilian. 15 January 1861, 5 February 1861.

The Groesbeck Journal (Texas). 15 May 1936.

Houston Telegraph and Texas Register (Texas). 27 July 1842.

Oklahoma City Daily Oklahoman. 26 June 1957.

Washington-on-the-Brazos Texas National Register. 26 June 1845.

Secondary Sources

Books and Dissertations

Bedford, H. G. *Texas Indian Troubles*. Dallas: Hargreaves Printing Co., 1905.

Bandelier, Adolph F. *Southwestern Journals of Adolph F. Bandelier*. Edited by Charles J. Lange and Carroll L. Riley. Albuquerque: University of New Mexico Press, 1966.

Brenner, Judith Ann. "Lone Star Soldier: A Study of the Military Career of Lawrence Sullivan Ross." Ph. D. diss., Texas Christian University, 1975.

_____. *Sul Ross: Soldier, Statesman, Educator*. College Station: Texas A & M University Press, 1983.

Brown, John Henry. *Indian Wars and Pioneers of Texas*. Austin: L. E. Daniell, 1880.

Brown, Mary M. *A Condensed History of Texas for Schools*. . . . N.p.: 1895.

DeShields, James T. *Border Wars of Texas*. Tioga, Tex.: Herald Company, 1912.

_____. *Cynthia Ann Parker: The Story of Her Capture*. St. Louis: 1886; repr., New York: Garland, 1976.

Dobie, J. Frank. *On the Open Range*. Dallas: Southwest Press, 1931.

Fallwell, Gene. *The Comanche Trail of Thunder and the Massacre at Parker's Fort*. Dallas: Highlands Historical Press, 1958.

Fehrenbach, T. R. *Comanches*. New York: Alfred A. Knopf, 1979.

Graves, John A., and Fred R. Cotten. *Home Place*. N.p.: Pioneer Texas Heritage Committee, 1958.

Gulick, Charles Adams, ed. *The Papers of Mirabeau Buonaparte Lamar*. Austin: Von Boeckmann-Jones Co., 1924.

Hagan, William T. *United States-Comanche Relations: The Reservation Years*. New Haven: Yale University Press, 1976.

Haley, J. Evetts. *Charles Goodnight: Cowman and Plainsman*. Norman: University of Oklahoma Press, 1949.

Jackson, Grace. *Cynthia Ann Parker*. San Antonio: Naylor Publishing, 1959.

Keating, Bern. *An Illustrated History of the Texas Rangers*. Chicago: Rand McNally & Co., 1975.

Ledbetter, Barbara A. Neal. *Fort Belknap, Frontier Saga*. Burnet, Tex.: Eakin Press, 1982.

Marcy, Randolph Barnes. *Thirty Years of Army Life on the Border*. New York: Harper and Brothers, 1866.

A Memorial and Biographical History of Navarro, Henderson, Anderson, Limestone, Freestone and Leon Counties, Texas. Chicago: Lewis Publishing Co., 1893.

Neighbours, Kenneth F. *Robert Simpson Neighbors and the Texas Frontier, 1836-1859*. Waco: Texian Press, 1978.

Newcomb, W. W., Jr. *The Indians of Texas*. Austin: University of Texas Press, 1978.

Paddock, Buckley B., ed. *A Twentieth Century History and Biographical Record of North and West Texas*. New York: Lewis Publishing Co., 1906.

Paine, Albert. *Captain Bill McDonald, Texas Ranger*. New York: J. J. Little & Ives, 1909.

Parker, James W. *Narrative of the perilous adventures, miraculous escapes and sufferings of Rev. James W. Parker. . ..* Louisville, Ky.: Morning Courier Office, 1844.

Plummer, Rachel. *The Rachel Plummer Narrative*. Louisville, Kentucky: Morning Courier Office, 1844; repr., Palestine, Tex.: 1926.

_____. *Rachel Plummer's Narrative of 21 Months Servitude as a Prisoner Among the Comanche Indians*. Houston: Telegraph Power Press, 1838; repr., Austin: Jenkins Publishing Press, 1977.

Richardson, Rupert N. *The Comanche Barrier to South Plains Settlement*. Glendale, Calif.: Arthur H. Clark Co. 1933.

_____. *The Frontier of Northwest Texas, 1846 to 1876*. Glendale, Calif.: Arthur J. Clark Co., 1963.

Rister, Carl Coke. *Border Captives: The Traffic in Prisoners by Southern Plains Indians, 1835 — 1875*. Norman: University of Oklahoma Press, 1940.

_____. *Fort Griffin on the Texas Frontier*. Norman: University of Oklahoma Press, 1956.

Robertson, Pauline Durrett, and R. L. Robertson. *Panhandle Pilgrimage*. Amarillo: Paramount Publishing Co., 1978.

Tolbert, Frank X. *An Informal History of Texas*. New York: Harper & Brothers Publishers, 1961.

Waldraven-Johnson, Margaret. *White Comanche: The Story of Cynthia Ann Parker and her Son, Quanah*. New York: Comet Press, 1956.

Webb, Walter Prescott. *The Texas Rangers*. Austin: University of Texas Press, 1965.

Wellman, Paul I. *Glory, God, and Gold*. New York: Doubleday, 1954.

Williams, Amelia W., and Eugene C. Barker, eds. *The Writings of Sam Houston, 1813 — 1863. 8 vol.* Austin: University of Texas Press, 1938-1940.

52 • Southwestern Studies

Articles

Crimmins, Col. M. I. "Camp Cooper and Fort Griffin, Texas." *West Texas Historical Association Yearbook.* 17 (October 1941): 32-43.

Debo, Angie. "Cynthia Ann Parker," in Edward J. James, et al., eds, *Notable American Women.* 3 vol. Cambridge: Harvard University Press, 1972, 3: 15-16.

_____. "Two Graves in Oklahoma." *Harper's Magazine* 213 (December 1956): 64-66.

Elam, Earl Henry. "The Butler and Lewis Mission and Treaty of 1846." *West Texas Historical Association Yearbook* 46 (1970): 72-100.

Neighbours, Kenneth F. "Fort Belknap," in *Frontier Forts of Texas.* Introduction by Rupert N. Richardson. Waco: Texian Press, 1966, 1-25.

Richardson, Rupert N. "The Death of Nocona and the Recovery of Cynthia Ann Parker." *Southwestern Historical Quarterly* 1 (1942): 15-21.

Wellman, Paul I. "Cynthia Ann Parker." *Chronicles of Oklahoma* 12 (no. 2, 1934): 163-171.

Wynne, Mamie Folsom. "History Centers About Cynthia Ann Parker's Home," in Wooten, Mattie L. *Women Tell the Story of the Southwest.* San Antonio: Naylor Co., 1940, 120-25.